EVIDENCE
FOR THE
RAPTURE
AND ITS TIMING

ROD NICHOLS

Publishing Coordinator – Sharon Kizziah-Holmes
Cover Design – Jaycee DeLorenzo

Paperback-Press
an imprint of A & S Publishing
Paperback Press, LLC.
Springfield, Missouri

ISBN -13: 978-1-970560-04-6

ACKNOWLEDGMENTS

First, I want to acknowledge God for saving my life through the death of His Son, Jesus and for the new life I am now living, because of the resurrection of Christ.

Second, I want to thank my wife, Karen, for continued support and encouragement for my writing. She's my number one fan.

Third, I want to acknowledge some other authors and teachers who have contributed to my knowledge of the end times and rapture. These would include Lee W. Brainard, Ken Johnson, Tim LaHaye, Jeff Kinley, Todd Hampson, Mark Hitchcock, Amir Tsarfati, and David Jeremiah. I highly encourage you to read their books, as well.

I also want to thank my editor, Jenn Bateman, for her good work, Sharon Kizziah-Holmes at Paperback Press for her work in the professional layout of the book, and Jaycee DeLorenzo for her assistance with the cover design.

TABLE OF CONTENTS

PREFACE

When people ask me about my favorite book in the Bible, my answer is always Revelation. It captured me in 2001, when another pastor and I taught a series on the end times. Over the last two decades, I've read just about every book written about the end times. I've also studied Revelation multiple times each year. Why is it my favorite book of the Bible? Because it offers all believers hope in the knowledge of what is coming.

Haven't you thought that you'd like to know the future, so you could make some changes now? Professional football is another of my great loves. I grew up in Denver, so I'm a forever Bronco fan. Then I went to college and settled in Tacoma, WA, so I'm also a Seahawks fan. Now I live in the Phoenix area, and I've become a Cardinals fan. Ticket prices have gotten expensive, and the crowds are a bit crazier than they used to be, so I don't go to games often. I prefer to watch them on TV. With multiple camera angels, sky cam, and instant replay, football is better on TV. However, there have been times when I couldn't watch my favorite team and so I would record it and watch later. Unlike most people who do this, I love to know the outcome of the game before I watch the replay. That way, if it's a win, I can be excited all throughout the game and if it's a loss, I can pick and choose what and how long I watch.

I'm a bit like that with fiction books. I often read the final chapter before I start the book. I like to know the end before I start reading. That's what Revelation offers. Most of this amazing book is a prophecy about our future. You can read Revelation and know what is going to happen in our world. Plus, it has a happy ending for all those who believe in Jesus as their Savior. It's a terrible ending for those who reject Jesus and choose to go their own way. If you are one of those, reading Revelation will probably help you make the most important decision of your lifetime.

In this book, I'm only going to cover a small part of Revelation. You can learn more by reading my book Where Did All the People Go? That book also talks about the rapture, but I also introduce the reader to what happens after the church is raptured. Following this book will be a book titled Revelation De-Mystified, which will help readers understand the beautiful symbolism in the Revelation of Jesus Christ. Look for that book within a year or so.

If you are a believer in Jesus as your Savior, this book will open your eyes to the amazing future we have ahead of us and should give you tremendous hope in the middle of this crazy world filled with hopeless people.

The book is also a great tool for starting conversations about the coming world event, the rapture, which will hopefully lead your friends and family to know and receive Jesus.

Enjoy the book, my friend.

Rod

INTRODUCTION

The Apostle Paul received a letter from the church leaders in Thessalonica. Paul taught them about the end times and the rapture of the church, also known as the bride of Christ. Remarkably similar to the church today, many people had questions about how and when this would happen. Some were saying the rapture had already happened and they missed it. Paul, in 1 Thessalonians 4:13-18 comforts and assures them that they had not missed the rapture:

"Brothers and sisters, we do not want you to be uninformed about those who sleep in death, so that you do not grieve like the rest of mankind, who have no hope. For we believe that Jesus died and rose again, and so we believe that God will bring with Jesus those who have fallen asleep in him. According to the Lord's word, we tell you that we who are still alive, who are left until the coming of the Lord, will certainly not precede those who have fallen asleep. For the Lord himself will come down from heaven, with a loud command, with the voice of the archangel and with the trumpet call of God, and the dead in Christ will rise first. After that, we who are still alive and are left will be caught up together with them in the clouds to meet the Lord in the air. And so we will be with the Lord forever. Therefore encourage one another with these words."

Paul is clearly painting a picture of the future rapture of the church. We will dig into that set of scriptures later in the book.

Remember that Paul was not the first to teach about the rapture, Jesus was. Paul learned about the rapture of the church from Jesus. We know this by studying both John 14:1-3 and 1 Thessalonians 4:15 (that we just read, where Paul said, "according to the Lord's word"). We will also study these scriptures later. The key here is that the early church believed in and taught about the rapture.

Other early church leaders like the Shepherd of Hermas (AD 150), Irenaeus (AD 170), Hippolytus (AD 210), Victorinus (AD 240), Cyprian (AD 250), and Ephraim the Syrian (AD 373) not only taught about the rapture but taught the pre-tribulation rapture. We will examine some of their writings in a later chapter. Just this fact alone eliminates the idea that the rapture and all of what we see in Revelation happened around AD 70, according to some theories. I will further debunk this idea when we talk about Myths and Misinformation in chapter eleven.

So, why another book on the rapture of the church? Because in over twenty years of studying, I was unable to find a book that had all of what I considered to be irrefutable evidence for the pre-tribulation rapture. Also, I still find so many people who are confused about the rapture and when it will happen.

It saddens me that Jesus, Paul, and other early church leaders taught about the rapture and a pre-tribulation rapture at that, so why is there so much confusion? Because the author of confusion, the father of lies, satan/the devil is trying to confuse the church and cause division through differing beliefs. I'm hoping this book can cut through the confusion and bring clarity.

Father God gave us the pre-tribulation rapture message to give us hope and excitement for the future. It's been that way since the days of Jesus, the disciples, Paul, and the early church leaders. So, why would we want to believe something different? We shouldn't. Let's just believe in and trust God and go spread the Kingdom of God throughout the world.

When I started my end times journey, over twenty years ago, I too was not sure about the rapture and its placement in the timeline. After years of studying, I can without a shadow of a doubt say that I believe the church/bride will be raptured prior to the beginning of the seven-year tribulation. In the balance of this book, I will systematically lay out this evidence. I do this not to convince you, but so you can do your own research and come to a conclusion that you can stand on.

I want you to know that this is not an exhaustive study of the end times, rapture, or the pre-tribulation rapture. Also, I am not like many of the self-proclaimed theologians who fill Amazon and YouTube with their teaching, I'm just a fellow traveler with you. I'm sharing what I've learned, in hopes that it will excite you to do your own due diligence.

All that said, no one knows when the rapture will occur. Only Father God knows when He will send

Jesus back for His bride. With that in mind, we need to be ready and watching for our Bridegroom and Savior. I can't imagine that the church will be on earth during the tribulation, but if we must live through part or all of the tribulation, we should be ready. The study of scripture and time spent developing an intimate relationship with God will accomplish that. So, get ready, watch and expect Jesus to return any day.

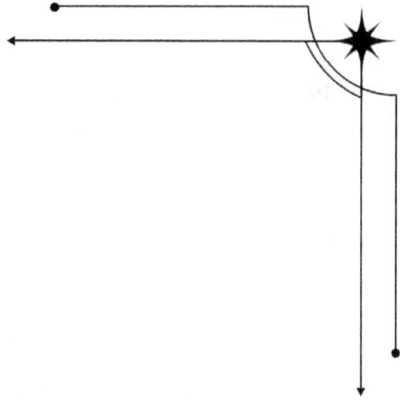

CHAPTER 1

WHY STUDY THE END TIMES AND THE RAPTURE?

#1 Scripture is Important

I believe that every word in the Bible is important to study. 2 Timothy 3:16-17 says, "All Scripture is God-breathed and is useful for teaching, rebuking, correcting and training in righteousness, so that the servant of God may be thoroughly equipped for every good work." If all scripture is breathed out of the mouth of God, then it is important. I always say that if you find something once in scripture, it's important to God and we should learn from it. Well, about 30% of the scriptures are prophetic, many are about the first coming of Jesus, all of which have been fulfilled. There are still many prophetic scriptures about Jesus returning. Since those about his first coming were 100% accurate, we can bank that those about His second coming will also be 100% accurate. Clearly, if God gave that much attention to the end times, we should too, but not at the expense of the rest of scripture.

The Bible is the most important book ever written and it has had more impact on humanity than any other book. It continues to be the best-selling book of all time. People are interested in knowing about God. The Bible is God's love letter to humankind. It's also His instruction manual for living this life. Finally, it's a historical document with 100% accuracy.

If you are wondering about the future of the world, your own future, and how everything turns out, read the Bible. It's not just in the book of Revelation. We find end times scriptures in the Old Testament books of Psalms, Isaiah, Ezekiel, Daniel, and others. Jesus talks about the end of days in Matthew 24 and 25, Mark 13, and Luke 21. Paul addresses it in 1 and 2 Thessalonians, 1 Corinthians 15, 1 Timothy 4, and 2 Timothy 3. Dr. Luke teaches about it in Acts 17. Peter covers the end times in 2 Peter 3. The end times and the rapture of the church are well covered topics in the scriptures.

#2 End Times Scripture Reveals God's Purpose

In the Genesis creation account, God forms the universe and our planet out of nothing. He literally speaks it into existence. Why? So, He could have a place for His ultimate creation – man and woman. He had millions of created angels at His beck and call, but He wanted a creature that could choose to love Him or not. God's purpose is revealed from the beginning of the Bible – to have a relationship with humankind. The whole middle section of the Bible is all about humans totally messing up God's plan. Even still, His purpose never changed and so we see, in the pre-tribulation rapture and end times scriptures, the fulfillment of God's plan to be with us forever.

The end times scriptures also introduce us to His ultimate relationship with us. The Father created, in the church, a bride for His Son. Contrary to popular belief, the church is not a building we go to on Saturday or Sunday or Wednesday. We, those who believe and have faith in Jesus as our Savior, comprise the church. That group of people is also referred to as Jesus' bride (see Ephesians 5:22-33, Revelation 19:7-9, and Revelation 21:1-2). One day soon, all the believers in Jesus (both dead and living) will be taken up into the sky to meet Jesus, the Bridegroom. We will be married to Him and rule with Him. That is our ultimate purpose.

#3 End Times Scriptures Help Us Understand the World Around Us

Have you ever wondered why there has always been so much attention on Israel. It's a country the size of New Jersey with only about ten million people living there. I live in Phoenix, AZ and there are over five million people here. So, we ask, "Why Israel?" Because the Jews are God's chosen people, the apple of His eye, and they play a huge role in the end times. By studying Revelation and other end times scriptures, we gain a better understanding of what is happening now in Israel and in the middle east and why. It helps us cut through all the confusion and brings a level of clarity to our world. Clarity eliminates confusion and the possibility of fear.

The end times scriptures also help us understand the world around us. For example, we notice the increase in the occurrence of storms, floods, and earthquakes in the past several years. When Adam and Eve sinned against God, the earth was cursed. It's that curse we are feeling. Paul teaches about this in Romans 8:22-24, "We know that the whole creation has been groaning as in the pains of childbirth right up to the present time. Not only so, but we ourselves, who have the first fruits of the Spirit, groan inwardly as we wait eagerly for our adoption to sonship, the redemption of our bodies. For in this hope, we were saved. But hope that is seen is no hope at all. Who hopes for what they already have?"

If you know anything about childbirth, the pains grow more intense and closer together as the birth approaches. That is what's happening in our world. All of what we see around us is birth pains preceding the birth of the new heaven and earth that we see in Revelation 21. Not only is creation groaning but so are all the believers who are awaiting our official salvation, adoption, and our new heavenly bodies. This is where we get our hope from, but right now it's hope based on faith. One day soon there will be a shout from heaven (I believe that it's Jesus saying "Come Up") and a trumpet blast. The dead in Christ will go up first and then those believers who are still alive, will rise to join them in the sky to meet Jesus. This is the rapture.

Understanding the end times also helps us recognize why there is so much governmental turmoil. The world is getting ready for the King of kings, the Lord of lords to return to earth to establish His Kingdom and Rule. This means that there is a lot going on in the heavenly realm that we can't see, but we can feel. Satan and his minions are fighting against this happening, but they won't win. We've read the end of the book. We will win!

The end times scriptures, particularly those about the pre-tribulation rapture are incredibly important to the church, as it shows us our wonderful future. There is no bad news for the believers in Jesus.

#4 The Bible is All About the End Times

So many people think that eschatology, the study of the end times, is a relatively new study, but it actually dates back thousands of years to the day of the fall in the Garden of Eden. As a part of the serpent's (satan's) punishment, God said in Genesis 3:15, "And I will put enmity between you and the woman, and between your offspring and hers; he will crush your head, and you will strike his heel." Enmity means a mutual hatred, so there would be a mutual hatred between satan and the woman (Israel) and between your offspring (those who choose to follow the devil) and her offspring (Jews). We see this often throughout history, as there has never been a more persecuted people group than the Jews. This prophecy also extends into the end times where we see the woman's ultimate offspring, Jesus. He conquered satan's legal plan to destroy God's children because of sin. Jesus will conquer satan and his followers once and for all at the end of the tribulation in battle of Armageddon.

God gave many of the Old Testament prophets words of prophecy about the end times. Daniel (Daniel 9) was given the seventy-week prophecy (seventy sets of seven years or 490 years), which includes the final seven years of the tribulation. Daniel was also shown a picture of the abomination of desolation that will happen in the middle of the tribulation when the antichrist sets up a talking statue in the middle of the newly built Jewish temple in Jerusalem.

Zechariah (11:15-17) also received prophetic visions and words about the antichrist who will take power at the beginning of the tribulation. Ezekiel received a prophetic picture of a battle, known as the Gog and Magog war that will likely happen between the rapture of the church and the beginning of the seven-year tribulation (Ezekiel 38 & 39). These are just a few of the examples that are given in the Bible. This is one of the reasons I highly recommend that people read the whole Bible.

Jesus even told his disciples about the end times in Matthew 24, Mark 13, and Luke 21. Jesus taught them about the rapture in John 14:1-3, "Do not let your hearts be troubled. You believe in God; believe also in me. My Father's house has many rooms; if that were not so, would I have told you that I am going there to prepare a place for you? And if I go and prepare a place for you, I will come back and take you to be with me that you also may be where I am." Jesus is referencing a traditional Jewish wedding process that I will discuss in greater detail later in the book. Spoiler alert: If you are a believer in and follower of Jesus, then you are His bride, and He is your bridegroom. You are betrothed. A big part of the end times story is an epic wedding.

Then, of course, we have the book of Revelation, which is mostly about the end times. The end of the church age, rapture of the church/bride, seven-year tribulation, and the return of Jesus with His believers to the earth to rule for a thousand years. Our home will be in heaven, but we will rule with Jesus on a newly formed earth. Then, we see the big moment- the final battle on earth followed by our heavenly home coming from the sky to a new earth and we will live there in paradise forever.

#5 We Are to Be Informed

In 1 Thessalonians 4:13, the Apostle Paul says, "Brothers and sisters, we do not want you to be uninformed…" He goes on from there to talk about the rapture of the church. I struggle when I meet Christians and even Pastors who say they aren't sure what they believe about the rapture. Some even say they are "pan-trib," which means that they don't care enough to do their due diligence and see what the Bible says. Instead, they just figure everything will pan out and Jesus will come back. That's an example of being uninformed and they are choosing to remain that way. If that's you, then I hope this book will motivate you to study the Bible and align yourself with what the Bible (not me or anyone else) says about the rapture and the end times.

God has given us the Bible, so that we can be informed. Why is that important? Because we are His messengers on earth. We must be able to help new Christians become informed. That's called discipleship.

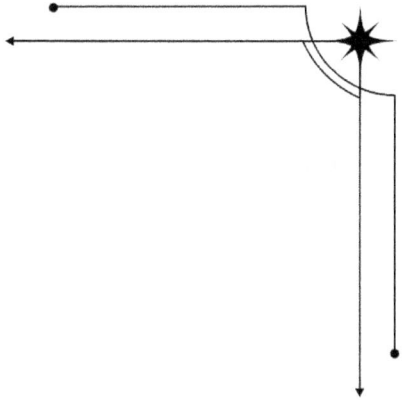

CHAPTER 2

WHAT IS THE RAPTURE?

If you do a word study in the Bible, you will not find the word rapture. That doesn't mean it doesn't exist. The word Bible also isn't in the Bible and yet we know it exists. So, if the word rapture isn't there, how do we know about it? The Apostle Paul talks about the rapture in 1 Thessalonians 4:13-18, which was referenced in the introduction. Let's read it again:

> *"Brothers and sisters, we do not want you to be uninformed about those who sleep in death, so that you do not grieve like the rest of mankind, who have no hope. For we believe that Jesus died and rose again, and so we believe that God will bring with Jesus those who have fallen asleep in him. According to the Lord's*

word, we tell you that we who are still alive, who are left until the coming of the Lord, will certainly not precede those who have fallen asleep. For the Lord himself will come down from heaven, with a loud command, with the voice of the archangel and with the trumpet call of God, and the dead in Christ will rise first. After that, we who are still alive and are left will be caught up together with them in the clouds to meet the Lord in the air. And so we will be with the Lord forever. Therefore encourage one another with these words."

The key phrase is "caught up together." The English versions of the New Testament were translated from Greek and so the word that was translated as "caught up" is harpazo (which is pronounced "har-pad-zo"). It means to seize, carry off by force, or snatch out or away. Harpazo is used in Acts 8:39, "When they came up out of the water, the Spirit of the Lord suddenly took Philip away, and the eunuch did not see him again, but went on his way rejoicing." This verse describes that the Lord suddenly took Philip away, snatching him out of the water. The word, harpazo was also used in 2 Corinthians 12:2, "I know a man in Christ who fourteen years ago -whether in the body I do not know, or out of the body I do not know, God knows - such a man was caught up to the third heaven." These last two examples of harpazo are also examples or shadows of the rapture of the church.

So, how do we get from harpazo to rapture? That's a good question and one that has an answer.

It comes from the Latin Vulgate translation of the Bible. One Latin word for caught up is rapturo. This is where we get our English word, rapture. So, when people say that the rapture isn't in the Bible, they are incorrect.

The next question you may be asking is who is raptured? Paul answers this in both 1 Thessalonians 4:13 and 1 Corinthians 15:50. Both scriptures are about the rapture, and he starts both with "brothers and sisters," so he is writing to fellow believers in Jesus Christ. A believer is someone who has believed in their heart and confessed out of their mouth that Jesus is their personal Savior. So, it's believers in Jesus who are raptured, and they are referred to many times in the New Testament as the church (Matthew 18:15 & 17, Acts 5:11, Acts 8:1 & 3, Acts 9:31, Acts 11:19, just to name a few). So, we can say that it's the church that is raptured. The Bible also refers to believers as the bride of Christ, so it's Jesus taking His bride out of harm's way. (More on this later in the book.)

Now, you might be wondering why the church is raptured and that would be another good question. I will get into more detailed explanations in the following chapters, but a quick reason is that Father God is taking His church, His kids, and His Son's bride away before He pours out His wrath on the earth. This is His nature all through the Bible. We see this in Genesis 19:16, "But he hesitated. So, the men seized his hand and the hand of his wife and the hands of his two daughters, for the compassion of the LORD was upon him; and they brought him out and put him outside the city." Lot was the only righteous man in Sodom and the angels had to take him out of the city before God destroyed it. The Lord could not bring His wrath on the sinful city until the righteous man was taken away.

Another example that it's God's nature to rapture (take away) the righteous before pouring out His wrath is the story of Noah. Noah was a godly man and a prophet. God came to him and said, "I am going to put an end to all people, for the earth is filled with violence because of them. I am surely going to destroy both them and the earth. So, make yourself an ark of cypress wood; make rooms in it and coat it with pitch inside and out." (Genesis 6:13-14) Many theologians believe that it took at least 75 years for Noah to build the ark and all the while, he warned the people about the impending flood. Unfortunately, when the day came for God to seal Noah and his family in the ark, no one else joined them. When the floods came, the ark carried them on the flood waters that were up high above the mountains. Once again, the righteous were taken up and out of harm's way, as God poured out His wrath on the sinful world.

For nearly two thousand years, the church has been warning people about the impending rapture. One day soon, without any warning, Jesus will call for His bride, the church to come meet Him in the clouds and they will be with Him forever. As it is written in both the stories of Lot and Noah, the reason for the rapture is that God is going to pour out His full wrath on those who remain on the earth during a seven-year period called the tribulation. The book of Revelation describes what happens during the tribulation in chapters 6-18. It is the most horrific time in earth's history. Most of the remaining population will be killed. However, God will spare His righteous ones by taking them out of the world.

You might be wondering what that will look like. No one knows for sure, but we do know, based on Paul's description in 1 Corinthians 15:52, it will be "in a flash, in the twinkling of an eye." The time for a twinkling would be the time it takes for light to travel through the lens of the eye and reflect off the retina. Light travels 186,000 miles per second. I've never been much for math, but I can tell this is going to be very quick. There are pictures and movies of people floating up into the sky, and while that is cool and dramatic, it is not accurate. What will more likely happen is that in one moment, you are here on earth and in the next, you are gone. I am glad we aren't floating into the sky, as I have a strong fear of heights. God must have known.

As of 2023, there are an estimated 2.4 billion Christians, which represents about 31.2% of the earth's human population. It's hard to imagine that many people disappearing at one time. However, it is easy to imagine the chaos it will cause. People driving cars, buses, trucks, trains, and flying airplanes will just disappear. It will truly be the biggest world-changing event in history.

The rapture is referred to as an imminent event, which means that it could happen any time. There are no warning signs. There is nothing that needs to happen before the rapture. It could literally happen any minute, which means we need to be ready. If you have not received Jesus as your Savior, you need to do that right now. For the rest of us, we are to watch for Jesus, preach the gospel, and make more disciples. God would love it if everyone went in the rapture.

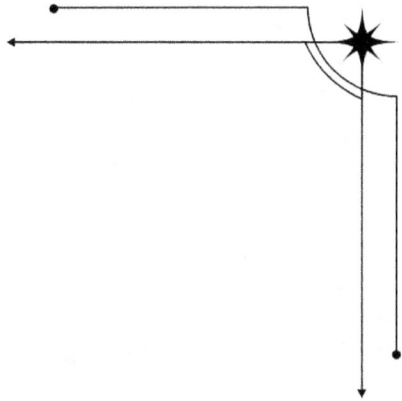

CHAPTER 3

RAPTURE TIMING THEORIES

Most Christians believe in a rapture, but not all agree on the timing. There are four timing theories. In this chapter, I'm going to cover all four and then talk about the one that fits the best biblically, fits the Jewish wedding narrative that Jesus spoke of, and best fits God's nature and relationship with humankind.

Theory 1 – Post-Tribulation Rapture

The post-tribulation theory says that the church will be raptured into heaven at the end of the seven-year tribulation and will then do a U-turn and come back with Jesus when He returns to earth.

There are several issues with this theory. First, the rapture is typically portrayed as an imminent event, which means it could happen at any time.

Matthew 24:42 reads, "Therefore keep watch, because you do not know on what day your Lord will come." 1 Thessalonians 5:2 says, "for you know very well that the day of the Lord will come like a thief in the night." Revelation 16:15, "Behold, I am coming like a thief! Blessed is the one who stays awake, keeping his garments on, that he may not go about naked and be seen exposed!" Many theories out there suggest that this refers to Jesus returning at the end of the tribulation. If that is the case, then we know exactly when he is going to return. This doesn't seem to work with the idea of an imminent return. Post-tribulationists argue that Jesus' imminent return is within a season, but this isn't accurate because we can easily see the events of the last half of the tribulation and once the tribulation begins, it's easy to calculate the number of days.

Secondly, those who believe in the post-tribulation rapture say that the rapture and the second coming are the same event and yet scripture very clearly describes two different events. Let's examine Zechariah 14:3-4, "Then the Lord will go out and fight against those nations, as he fights on a day of battle. On that day his feet will stand on the Mount of Olives, east of Jerusalem, and the Mount of Olives will be split in two from east to west, forming a great valley, with half of the mountain moving north and half moving south." This describes Jesus returning to and setting foot on earth, then going out to fight the end time armies. This is contrasted with 1 Thessalonians 4:16-17, "For the Lord himself will come down from heaven, with a loud command, with the voice of the archangel and with the trumpet call of God, and the dead in Christ will rise first. After that, we who are still alive and are left will be caught up together with them in the clouds to meet the Lord in the air. And so we will be with the Lord forever." Here we see Jesus stopping in mid-air, dead and alive believers rise up to meet him and go to be with him. He never sets foot on the earth. That causes a logistical nightmare that is hard for post-tribulationists to explain.

Thirdly, it requires the church, Jesus' bride, to endure the wrath of Jesus/Lamb in the first half of the tribulation and then the Father's wrath in the second half. The scriptures make it clear that Jesus died on the cross once and for all the sin of humanity. The Father put all the sin of humankind on the sinless Son and then poured out all the stored-up wrath on Him. The Father has no more wrath to pour out on the church, so the church could not possibly be there during the tribulation.

Also, why would our loving Bridegroom allow His bride to suffer through the most horrific time in earth's history? Why would our loving Father allow His kids to suffer His wrath. Now, some out there will say, but many people will receive Christ during the tribulation and yet they have to endure His Wrath. These are all people who were warned about the coming rapture and made the choice to miss it. That said, I'm sure that God causes the suffering to be short for those who receive Christ during the tribulation, and they are then taken to heaven to be with Him forever.

The fourth reason is that in Titus 2:13, the apostle Paul refers to Christ's return as the "blessed hope." How could believers suffering through the horrific tribulation be considered the blessed hope? Those who support the post-tribulation theory say that suffering, hardship, and persecution are just part of life as a Christian. That may be true, but the seven-year tribulation is God pouring His wrath out on the earth, which is way beyond typical suffering in this life.

The other pieces of the picture that are missing in the post-tribulation theory are the BEMA judgement, which is a rewards judgment for believers (See Romans 14:10 and 2 Corinthians 5:10). 1 Corinthians 3:12-15 describes what will happen at this judgement. Everything we have done during our earthly life will be laid on the heavenly altar. Holy Fire will burn off the wood, hay, and stubble – all the worldly stuff we did and acquired, or the things God wanted us to do, but we didn't do them. However, the fire will leave gold, silver, and precious stones – all the things we did to spread the Kingdom of God on earth and to take care of God's kids in need. I believe that Jesus will use the gold, silver, and precious stones to craft crowns that we will receive as a gift to worship Jesus (see Revelation 4:10). Then a question arises, if the church is doing a quick U-turn, when does this occur?

There are many out there who believe in the post-tribulation rapture, but I find most of them have never really studied what the Bible has to say about the end times and rapture. I believe they are carrying a deception passed on from one person to another. I don't see any solid biblical evidence for the post-tribulation rapture. It also doesn't fit the nature or character of God. We should always interpret scripture in context with other scripture. When we do that, we see God pulling the righteous people out before He pours out His wrath. A post-tribulation rapture does not fit God's nature and character, nor does it fit biblical context.

Theory 2 – Mid-Tribulation Rapture

This theory has the church raptured at the mid-point (3-1/2 years) of the tribulation. They argue that the church must be raptured before the wrath of God begins, but that the wrath in the first half of the tribulation is from man and satan. This is quickly proven to be false by examining Revelation 6:16-17, "They called to the mountains and the rocks, 'Fall on us and hide us from the face of him who sits on the throne and from the wrath of the Lamb! For the great day of their wrath has come, and who can withstand it?'" Did you catch that? The wrath of the Lamb. Who is the Lamb? It's Jesus. So, the wrath poured out through the seven seal judgements is the wrath of Jesus. But wait, there's more. It also said, "hide us from the face of him who sits on the throne AND the wrath of the Lamb." Who sits on the throne and isn't Jesus? God the Father. So, this is clearly God's wrath during the first part of the tribulation, not the wrath of man or satan.

So, as with the post-tribulation rapture theory, why would the Father want His Son's bride to suffer through even half of His wrath on the earth?

Also, is that even possible, considering He poured out all the wrath the church deserved on Jesus when he hung on the cross? The answer is no. That would be double wrath on the church and that does not fit God's promise for salvation.

The mid- and post-tribulation theories also have a hard time explaining why the church is mentioned in Revelation chapters 1-3, but disappears in chapters 4-18, only to reappear with Jesus in chapter 19. This seems like an easy explanation. Chapters 1-3 represent letters to actual churches, but they also represent the church age or the age of grace. This ends in 4:1 with the church taken into heaven (with a shout and trumpet, just like in 1 Thessalonians 4:16) and then coming back with Jesus in Revelation 19:14, "The armies of heaven were following him, riding on white horses and dressed in fine linen, white and clean." How do we know this is the church and not angels? Let's go back to verses 6-8, "Then I heard what sounded like a great multitude, like the roar of rushing waters and like loud peals of thunder, shouting: 'Hallelujah!' For our Lord God Almighty reigns. Let us rejoice and be glad and give him glory! For the wedding of the Lamb has come, and his bride has made herself ready. Fine linen, bright and clean, was given her to wear." The bride is always a reference for the church, and we see that the bride is wearing fine linen, the same way those riding with Jesus are described in verse 14. We might say that the church, the bride, is wearing wedding clothes.

Lastly, the mid-tribulation theory is a recent theory developed in the 19th century. It does not have solid historical support from the early church leaders, like the pre-tribulation rapture does.

Theory 3 – Pre-Wrath Rapture

This theory teaches that the rapture of the church will occur somewhere in the middle of the second half of the tribulation, before God's final wrath is poured out. This is the most recent of the theories, as it was introduced in the 1970's by Robert Van Kampen and Marv Rosenthal. It was initially a fringe theory, but through the years has connected with some Christian circles.

The biggest issue with this theory is that it is completely new. I could find no evidence of early church fathers believing in a pre-wrath rapture. As best I could tell, no one believed this until the 1970's. That's a red flag to me.

Another issue I see is that the proponents of the pre-wrath rapture believe that the seven seal and seven bowl judgements were not God's wrath. I discussed this in the mid-tribulation rapture section earlier. Revelation 6:16-17 clearly states that the opening of the seals is the wrath of the Lamb and the Father. In my thinking, that's the wrath of God and it starts at the beginning of the seven-year tribulation. Usually, the pre-wrath people will argue that the wrath in the first two thirds of the tribulation is the wrath of man and satan, but again, Revelation 6:16-17 disproves this.

Another issue I have with this and all of the rapture theories except the pre-tribulation theory is that Jesus said, in Matthew 24, that the timing of His return will be like the days of Noah. They will be eating and drinking, marrying, and giving in marriage. This sounds to me like normal life and the middle to the end of the tribulation will be anything but normal life. In order for the rapture to happen in a time like the days of Noah, it must come before the antichrist comes into power and the tribulation begins.

Pre-wrath removes immanence, as it requires signs to occur (e.g., emergence of the antichrist, the abomination). As we see in Titus 2:13, Philippians 3:20, and 1 Thessalonians 1:10, the early church believed in the imminent return of Christ:

- ✓ Titus 2:12-13, "It teaches us to say "No" to ungodliness and worldly passions, and to live self-controlled, upright and godly lives in this present age, while we wait for the blessed hope—the appearing of the glory of our great God and Savior, Jesus Christ,"
- ✓ Philippians 3:20, "But our citizenship is in heaven. And we eagerly await a Savior from there, the Lord Jesus Christ,"
- ✓ 1 Thessalonians 1:10, "and to wait for his Son from heaven, whom he raised from the dead—Jesus, who rescues us from the coming wrath."

If the early church knew that the antichrist had to come and set up the abomination in the temple, why would they be waiting for the blessed hope – the appearing of the glory, the Savior, the Son from heaven, at that time. Instead, they would be looking for the antichrist to arise, but the early church leaders didn't teach them to look for the antichrist to be revealed. Plus, the end of 1 Thessalonians 1:10 clearly says that Jesus will rescue us (believers/church/bride) from the coming wrath. Now, the pre-wrath people will say that this wrath is eternity in hell, but if we examine the Greek word, which is orge, it's the same word used in Revelation 6:16-17 referring to the wrath of the Lamb and the great day of their wrath.

The pre-wrath people have to work hard at reordering the end-time events and redefining the tribulation and the Day of the Lord, in order to make their theory work. Critics of this theory say that this undermines the clarity of end times prophecy and forces man-made interpretation.

Theory 4 – Pre-Tribulation Rapture

After over twenty years of studying the end times scriptures, this is the only theory that fits biblically, culturally, and matches the nature and character of God. This theory has the rapture occurring before the revealing of the antichrist, his negotiation of a treaty with Israel, and the beginning of the seven-year tribulation. In the balance of this book, I will lay out the evidence for a pre-tribulation rapture and discuss the arguments against it.

Theory 5 – Pan-Tribulation Rapture

I'm going to add a fifth theory, because I run into some who believe in the pan-tribulation rapture. That it's all going to pan out. What they are really saying is that they don't want to invest the time to study the bible and produce a belief that they can share with others. That's just spiritual laziness. Don't be a pan-tribulation person.

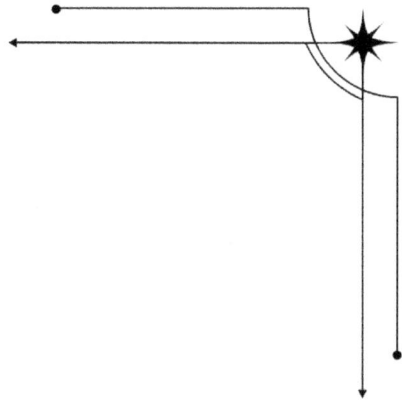

CHAPTER 4

HISTORICAL SUPPORT FOR THE PRE-TRIB RAPTURE

There is a stream of the church that is promoting the lie that the pre-tribulation rapture was invented by John Darby in the 1830's and that he was influenced by Margaret MacDonald's end time visions. However, Darby wrote about a pre-tribulation rapture before MacDonald's visions. Also, there is no documented evidence that Darby ever met MacDonald. Lastly, those who have carefully analyzed MacDonald's end times visions say that her statements align more closely with the post-tribulation theory.

The truth is that many of the early church leaders, during the first few centuries after Jesus ascended into heaven, taught a pre-tribulation rapture. Here are a few examples from a book titled *The Rapture*, written by Ken Johnson, ThD:

- ✓ **The Shepherd of Hermas** – around AD 150 wrote, "Go therefore and declare to the Elect of the Lord His mighty deeds and say to them that this beast is a type of the great tribulation which is to come. If ye therefore prepare yourselves and with your who heart turn to the Lord in repentance, then shall ye be able to escape it, if your heart is pure and blameless…the golden color stands for you who have escaped from this world…Now ye know the symbol of the great tribulation to come. But if ye are willing, it shall be nothing."
- ✓ **Irenaeus** – around AD 170 wrote, "When in the end that church will suddenly be caught up from this, then it is said, 'There will be tribulation such as not been since the beginning, nor will be.'" (Against Heresies 5.29)
- ✓ **Ephraim the Syrian** – around AD 373 wrote, "because all saints and the elect of the LORD are gathered together before the Tribulation, which is about to come and be taken to the LORD." (On the Last Times 2)

In his book, *Recent Pre-Trib Findings In the Early Church Fathers*, Theologian and Greek Scholar, Lee Brainard presents recent discoveries of pretribulation passages: ten from Ephraim the Syrian, nine from Eusebius, four from Irenaeus, and three from the Didache. Here is another quote from an early church father that supports that the pre-tribulation rapture was taught many, many years before Darby:

- ✓ **Eusebius** – born AD 260 to 265 and died AD 339-340, wrote "For the world shall meet with a great test in the season of apostasy, in which the faithful man will scarcely be found. Suddenly, there shall not even be one, because some have been taken and others left behind, delivered to the eagles." Eusebius also wrote (teaching on Luke 17:26), "As all perished then except those gathered with Noah in the ark, so also at his coming, the ungodly in the season of apostasy … shall perish … while … according to the pattern of Noah … all the righteous and godly are to be separated from the ungodly and gathered into the heavenly ark of God. For in this way [comes the time] when not even one righteous man will be found any more among mankind. And when all the ungodly have been made atheists by the antichrist, and the whole world is overcome by apostasy, the wrath of God shall come upon the ungodly."
- ✓ **Ephraim the Syrian,** "For the elect shall be gathered prior to the tribulation, so they shall not see the confusion and the great tribulation coming upon the unrighteous world."

Dr. William Watson, Professor of History at Colorado Christian College has published multiple articles with evidence of church leaders in the 16th and 17th centuries that taught pre-tribulation rapture. He also addresses this subject in Chapter seven of his book *Dispensationalism Before Darby*. Obviously, all of this is before John Nelson Darby in the 1830's, so those who are teaching that Darby invented the pre-tribulation rapture are incorrect, which means we also must consider whether anything they are teaching is true.

Although Jesus doesn't directly teach the pre-tribulation rapture, it sure sounds like it in Luke 21:34-36 (NASB 1995), "Be on guard, so that your hearts will not be weighted down with dissipation and drunkenness and the worries of life, and that day will not come on you suddenly like a trap; for it will come upon all those who dwell on the face of all the earth. But keep on the alert at all times, praying that you may have strength to escape all these things that are about to take place, and to stand before the Son of Man." Later, when Jesus appears to John and gives him what we know as the book of Revelation, Jesus says (in Revelation 3:10), "Since you have kept my command to endure patiently, I will also keep you from the hour of trial that is going to come on the whole world to test the inhabitants of the earth."

Jesus also taught about the pre-tribulation rapture in Matthew 24. Actually, Jesus talks about both His return and the rapture in that chapter. In verses 9-35, Jesus talks about the tribulation and His return to the earth. Verse 10 talks about the rebellion or falling away we just saw in Paul's teaching in 2 Thessalonians 2:3 NKJV, "Let no one deceive you by any means; for that Day will not come unless the falling away comes first, and the man of sin is revealed, the son of perdition."

In Matthew 24:15 Jesus talks about the abomination that causes desolation. This happens at the mid-point of the tribulation when the antichrist sets himself up in the third Jewish temple and declares himself as God. At this point, the Jews begin to flee Jerusalem, which we see in verses 16-21. We know these people are Jews, because it mentions the Sabbath and the church does not strictly observe the Sabbath. In verse 22, Jesus says that if God does not cut the tribulation short, all humankind would be destroyed. That's how bad it will be during these seven years.

Then in verses 27-30 Jesus describes what happens when He returns to the earth. All the people, who did not believe in Him, mourn as they see Him coming to earth from heaven. In verse 31, Jesus sends his angels with a loud trumpet call to gather the elect. This is a term that consistently is used for a believer in Jesus. Some people try to say that this is the rapture of the church, but it's more likely referring to those who become believers during the tribulation.

Now, let's move on to Matthew 24:36-51 where Jesus talks about the rapture of the church. In verse 36 Jesus makes it very clear that no one except the Father knows when Jesus will come for the church, His bride. I will explain why this is in the sixth chapter of this book, as we compare the traditional Jewish wedding with the rapture. In verses 37-39 Jesus discusses what things will be like before the rapture. It will be like the days of Noah – immorality, impurity, wickedness, and no focus on God. Noah preached about God and the coming judgement for over 75 years and only he and his family entered the ark and were saved. Christians have been preaching about the rapture of the church for nearly 2000 years, and we will see how many actually go in the rapture.

Also, the days of Noah were a time of normal life – "eating and drinking, marrying and giving in marriage and they knew nothing about what would happen until the flood came and took them all away." The ark is a type and shadow of the rapture. Prior to pouring out His wrath on the earth, God offered a way out, but only eight people entered the ark. They were then lifted high above the earth on the waters of the flood. Some will try to say that the ark is a shadow of believers being protected during the tribulation, but if you study Revelation, you will quickly see that believers (those who receive Jesus as Savior during the tribulation) are not protected. Many of them will be killed for not taking the mark of the beast and worshipping the antichrist. The ark took the righteous out of judgement, as will the rapture, which means it must happen before the tribulation begins.

We see this in verses 40-41, "Two men will be in the field; one will be taken and the other left. Two women will be grinding with a hand mill; one will be taken and the other left. This clearly shows that just like the days of Noah, the righteous are taken and the unrighteous (those who have not received Jesus as their Savior) are left behind and submitted to the wrath of God. Then in verses 42-44 Jesus subtly gives us the timing. "Therefore, keep watch, because you do not know on what day your Lord will come. But understand this: If the owner of the house had known at what time of night the thief was coming, he would have kept watch and would not have let his house be broken into. So you also must be ready, because the Son of Man will come at an hour when you do not expect him." This must be referring to a time before the tribulation, because otherwise, He would have said for them to watch for the rebellion and the antichrist to be revealed. In this entire section Jesus is talking about the imminent coming of the Son of Man in the sky to receive His bride.

In verses 45-51 Jesus describes the time we are in. The master went away and left the servants in charge. The master has stayed away a long time, and the servants aren't looking for the master, they are misbehaving. One day soon, Jesus will return in an hour we don't expect (which can't be during the tribulation, or we would be expecting it). He will take those who are prepared and looking for Him and the rest will be left behind to either die and spend eternity in hell or suffer in the tribulation.

If you haven't received Jesus as your Savior or you have and you aren't following Him, then you will be among those left behind. So, if you are feeling convicted by that and are ready to give your life to Jesus, just say this simple prayer. "Jesus, I confess that I'm a sinner and am heading to eternity in hell. I recognize you as the Savior of the world and receive you as my Savior. I give you my life and will follow you all the rest of my days." If you prayed that with your whole heart, then you are saved and will either be taken up into the sky to meet Jesus during the rapture or die and go meet Jesus. Now, you are to follow Him by doing what He did. Study the gospels of Matthew, Mark, Luke, and John and model yourself after Jesus. Find a good Holy-Spirit filled, Bible teaching church, to connect with other believers. Begin to tithe, give, and serve. Get rid of the sin areas of your life and those activities that distract you from time in the Bible and prayer. Find a believer who will mentor you. This will help you stay on the right path.

Now, let's talk about what the Apostle Paul taught in 2 Thessalonians 2:1-8, "Concerning the coming of our Lord Jesus Christ and our being gathered to him, we ask you, brothers and sisters, not to become easily unsettled or alarmed by the teaching allegedly from us—whether by a prophecy or by word of mouth or by letter—asserting that the day of the Lord has already come. Don't let anyone deceive you in any way, for that day will not come until the rebellion occurs and the man of lawlessness is revealed, the man doomed to destruction. He will oppose and will exalt himself over everything that is called God or is worshiped, so that he sets himself up in God's temple, proclaiming himself to be God. Don't you remember that when I was with you, I used to tell you these things? And now you know what is holding him back, so that he may be revealed at the proper time. For the secret power of lawlessness is already at work; but the one who now holds it back will continue to do so till he is taken out of the way. And then the lawless one will be revealed, whom the Lord Jesus will overthrow with the breath of his mouth and destroy by the splendor of his coming."

First, we need to establish what is meant by the day of the Lord. Isaiah prophetically describes it in Isaiah 13:6 & 9, "Wait, for the day of the Lord is at hand! It will come as destruction from the Almighty ... Behold, the day of the Lord comes, cruel, with both wrath and fierce anger, to lay the land desolate; and He will destroy its sinners from it." This sure sounds to me like a description of the tribulation. Joel describes it this way (Joel 2:1), "Blow the trumpet in Zion, and sound an alarm in My holy mountain! Let all the inhabitants of the land tremble; for the day of the Lord is coming, for it is at hand." Again, this sounds very much like the tribulation. Most Bible scholars define the day of the Lord as the period that we think of as the seven-year tribulation, which begins when the antichrist negotiates a peace treaty in the middle east and ends when Jesus sets foot on the Mt of Olives.

Okay, now back to 2 Thessalonians 2:1-8 and let's analyze what Paul is saying about the rapture and its timing. In verse 1, it's clear that Paul is writing about the rapture – "being gathered to him." Then we see that someone has been teaching the Thessalonians that the day of the Lord has already begun. However, in verse 3 Paul clarifies the timing of the day of the Lord (which was established earlier as representing the seven-year tribulation) can only begin after the rebellion occurs and the man of lawlessness is revealed. First, let's deal with the rebellion. Some other translations use the word apostasy because the Greek word translated is apostasia, which means a falling away or defection, so what Paul is saying is that the day of the Lord cannot begin until there is a falling away or defection of believers or at least pseudo believers.

Next, we see that the day of the Lord cannot begin until the man of lawlessness is revealed. This is the antichrist. In verse 6, we see another event that must happen before the antichrist can be revealed to the world – that which is restraining lawlessness and the revealing of the lawless one must be removed. So, what is it that restrains lawlessness now? Christians. The church. All the true believers in Jesus, the church, His Bride, must be removed in order for the antichrist to be revealed and for lawlessness to be unleashed. That's the rapture of the church and since the tribulation cannot begin until the antichrist is revealed, it must be pre-tribulation.

So, to sum it up, Paul had previously taught the Thessalonians about the pre-tribulation rapture, but some other teachers had confused them with false teaching that they were already in the middle of the tribulation and had missed the rapture (see verse 5). Paul let them know that they were not in the tribulation and had not missed the rapture, because the rebellion had not yet occurred, and the man of lawlessness had not yet been revealed. The same is true today.

I think it's pretty clear that from the days of Jesus forward, the pre-tribulation rapture was taught and believed. But, if you are still not a believer, keep reading, because there is more evidence to come.

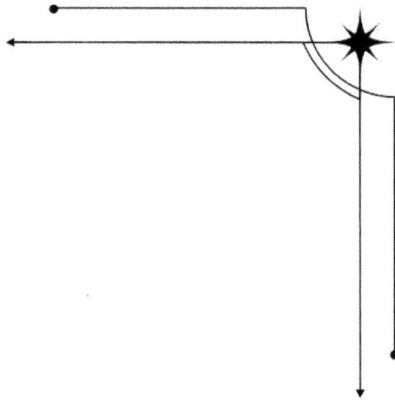

CHAPTER 5

NOT APPOINTED TO WRATH

I probably should have put this one first, because, in my mind, it's the biggest evidence of a pre-tribulation rapture. In 1 Thessalonians 5:9, Paul teaches, "For God did not appoint us to suffer wrath but to receive salvation through our Lord Jesus Christ." As discussed previously, the Greek word that is translated as wrath is orge, which means "anger exhibited in punishment hence used for punishment itself." This concept is then echoed in Revelation 3:10, as Jesus speaks to the church and says, "Since you have kept my command to endure patiently, I will also keep you from the hour of trial that is going to come on the whole world to test the inhabitants of the earth." Jesus is speaking about keeping the church from the coming tribulation. Notice that it's keeping from, rather than protecting in or during. Some people try to say that the church, the bride of Christ will go through all or parts of the tribulation with God's protection, but Jesus is very clear that He will keep the church from the hour of trial.

Because of sin, every person since Adam and Eve, have been deserving of the wrath of God. However, God loved us so much that He sent His only Son, Jesus, to shed his blood and die for our sins. Every person who has received Jesus as their Savior has been forgiven and no longer will be subjected to God's wrath. This includes His wrath during the seven-year tribulation, which is poured out on humanity because of sin. So, the quick and easy answer is that those who receive Jesus prior to the tribulation will be taken up into the sky to meet Jesus and will be with Him forever and those who receive Jesus during the tribulation will be protected from God's wrath (similar to the way the Jews were in Egypt during the ten plagues). Unfortunately, they will not be protected from man's wrath as many will be executed for not taking the mark of the beast.

Since we have lived in the church age or the age of grace all of our lives, you may be wondering why God would pour out His wrath during the tribulation. First, as was mentioned earlier, the sacrificial death of Jesus delt with sin once and for all, but salvation is a gift that must be received. During the age of grace, which will end when the church is taken up into heaven, the blood of Jesus in the church is holding back the wrath and also minimizing the lawlessness of man on earth. Once the church and its blood covering is removed, then both God's wrath and man's lawlessness will accelerate. God has been storing up wrath for nearly 2000 years for the millions of murders, abortions, sexual immorality, pornography, gender confusion, homosexuality, child trafficking, and our overall mocking of God and His commandments. All that stored up wrath will be poured out during the tribulation and you don't want to be there. Nor do you want any of your friends or family to experience that, so go and share the good news of Jesus and salvation with everyone you know and meet.

There are many out there who say that the wrath that Paul speaks of in 1 Thessalonians 5:9 is related only to salvation (saved from the wrath of God when we die) and not to the wrath poured out during the tribulation. I have a hard time understanding why they think this because God's wrath is God's wrath. It is always poured out because of sin or perhaps a better word would be rebellion.

All through the Old Testament, we see the Israelites rebelling against God and then are subjected to God's wrath. Here are a few examples:

- ✓ In Genesis 6, we see the great flood that destroys all of humankind, except Noah and his family, because of their sin/rebellion.
- ✓ In Genesis 19, we see God's wrath destroy the cities of Sodom and Gomorrah because of their sinfulness.
- ✓ In Exodus 7-12, we see God's wrath poured

out on Egypt because of Pharoah's rebellion against God.
- ✓ In Numbers 16, we see God's wrath when the earth opens and swallows Korah and those with him, because of rebellion.
- ✓ In Numbers 21, we see God's wrath when He sends poisonous snakes to kill the Israelites because of their rebellion.

These are just a few examples of God's wrath poured out on people in the time before Jesus came to earth and died for the sins of humanity. I don't know about you, but I'm so thankful for what Jesus did on the cross and that we, who believe, don't have to be subjected to God's horrible wrath.

Now, I want to take a moment to explain that God is not like a man/woman and His wrath is not anger in the way we think of anger. He's not mad at the person, He's angry with the sin in the person. Without Jesus' sacrifice on the cross for us, God would be angry with us too. The reason is that God is holy, and holiness and sin don't mix. Holiness kills sin, unless there is blood. In the Old Testament it was the blood of animals and in the New Testament, it is the blood of Jesus.

Okay, so if God's wrath is poured out because of the sin in people, but sin was dealt with for all believers on the cross of Calvary. Then how could God justify pouring it out again on believers? He could not. This takes us to the theological word propitiation, which is defined as the act of appeasing God's wrath through sacrifice, in particular the sacrifice of Jesus to bring us into right relationship with God. Earlier I mentioned that God is holy, and holiness and sin cannot exist together. Also, God is just and so sin must be dealt with through sacrifice or God will deal with it through His holy wrath.

Since God loved us so much, He sent His only son to be born a human, who would remain perfectly sinless and then die as the legal substitute for all humankind. Those who believe in and receive this sacrifice are saved from God's wrath (that's called grace). Those who don't will be subjected to that wrath. God doesn't choose who does and who doesn't, that's up to us. He gave us all free will, and we get to decide whether we accept God's gift of salvation given to us through His grace.

Everyone who has received Jesus as their Savior from the time of His death and resurrection forward will go up to meet Him in the sky and be with Him forever. That will mark the end of the church age or the age of grace. This is the time between when the Holy Spirit was poured out on believers on the day of Pentecost and the rapture; when Jesus takes His church out of the earth.

During the age of grace, the blood of Jesus holds back God's wrath. Even those who are not saved and living in blatant rebellion against God do not feel God's wrath until they die. As wonderful as this age is, it will one day end with the rapture of the church and then, even those who are saved during the tribulation will feel God's wrath all around them but not be subjected to it.

Let's look at a perfect example of this in

Revelation 16:2, "The first angel went and poured out his bowl on the land, and ugly, festering sores broke out on the people who had the mark of the beast and worshiped its image." Here we see that God only pours out His wrath on those who have taken the mark of the beast and worshiped its image, which will likely be most of those who have not yet received Jesus as their Savior. That said, those who have will be spared from this wrath.

There are some out there who try to teach that the wrath mentioned in 1 Thessalonians 5:9 and also in 1 Thessalonians 1:10, "and to wait for his Son from heaven, whom he raised from the dead—Jesus, who rescues us from the coming wrath" is just referring to eternal judgement (hell) and does not apply to the tribulation. This actually doesn't make any sense, because as I mentioned previously God's wrath is God's wrath. The timing doesn't matter. If believers in Jesus are not appointed to suffer wrath or rescued from wrath, this would mean they are both saved from eternal judgement and the judgement we see during the seven-year tribulation.

Another reason this doesn't make sense is that typically when the wrath of eternal judgement is mentioned it also includes descriptive terms like fire, darkness, wailing, and gnashing of teeth. We don't see these terms in either 1 Thessalonians 1:10 or 5:9, so although the wrath of eternal judgement would be included in these scriptures, so would the wrath poured out during the tribulation.

A final reason that this argument that this wrath is referring to eternal judgement doesn't make sense is that Paul would have already taught about salvation and believers would have understood that their sin was forgiven and they would not be subjected to God's wrath, so Paul was speaking of the wrath during the tribulation.

A final argument I often see against the idea that the church will be taken away before the wrath of God during the tribulation is that the first half of the tribulation is not God's wrath, but rather the wrath of man and satan. I mentioned this earlier in reference to some of the other rapture theories, but it's good to review. There is a quick and easy refute to this idea and all we have to do is look at Revelation 6:1, "I watched as the Lamb opened the first of the seven seals. Then I heard one of the four living creatures say in a voice like thunder, "Come!" 2 I looked, and there before me was a white horse! Its rider held a bow, and he was given a crown, and he rode out as a conqueror bent on conquest." This is a description of the antichrist being revealed and given authority by God to conquer through diplomacy (he has a bow, but no arrows, so he won't be a warrior) and it is the removing of the first seal by Jesus that releases him upon the world. The antichrist is an instrument of God's wrath.

If that isn't convincing enough, let's again look at Revelation 6:16-17, "They called to the mountains and the rocks, "Fall on us and hide us from the face of him who sits on the throne and from the wrath of the Lamb! 17 For the great day of their wrath has come, and who can withstand it?" This comes after the first six seals are opened by

Jesus, the Lamb and it's very clear that everything that happens with the opening of the first six seals is the wrath of the Lamb and God (Father).

The reason there is confusion over this is that most people think of God's wrath as always on full blast, but during the tribulation we see that it ramps up over the seven-year period. Each set of judgements – seals, trumpets, and bowls – are increasingly more destructive. Why? Because God is love and He would have no one perish. He is creating opportunities all throughout the tribulation for people to repent of their sin and receive Jesus as their Savior.

To conclude this evidential point, the rapture of the church must come before the tribulation begins, because that ends the age of God's grace. His wrath held back by the blood of Jesus, ends when the church is removed. If the church is removed at any other time than before the tribulation begins, then the church, Jesus' bride, would be subjected to the Father's wrath. During the tribulation God still offers the opportunity to repent and be saved, but His wrath will still pour out on the world, like the way it did in the Old Testament.

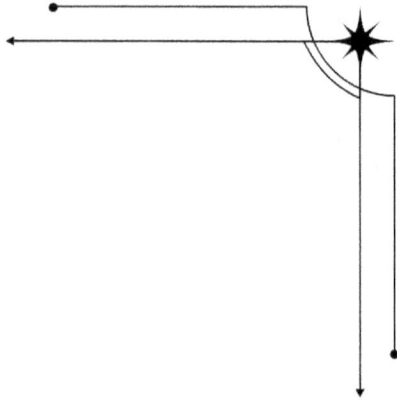

CHAPTER 6

THE CHURCH IN HEAVEN

This is another of the evidential proofs I could have led with. Although Revelation is not completely chronological, the early chapters are. Chapters two and three describe what we know as the church age or the age of grace. Although they are letters written to seven actual churches, some theologians teach that each letter represents a period of time in the church age. Let's examine each church and how it applies to a certain time frame in the development of the church:

- ✓ Ephesus represents the early church from Jesus' death and resurrection to about AD 100. This is the faithful church.
- ✓ Smyrna represents the period from AD 101 to around AD 313 which was a period of

heavy suffering and persecution for the church.

✓ Pergamos represents the time from AD 314 to AD 590 which was a time of great compromise because the church allowed the world to influence it. It was in AD 380 that Christianity became the official religion of the Roman Empire and the Holy Roman Catholic church was launched, and the church began meeting in buildings.

✓ Thyatira represents the time from AD 591 to 1517. It was a time of spiritual decline and compromise, as the culture continued to invade the church. It was also marked by an increase in false teaching.

✓ Sardis represents the time from AD 1518 to 1700 which was the beginning of the protestant reformation. It represents a period of spiritual awakening and revival.

✓ Philadelphia represents the time from AD 1701 to 1900 which was a period of great revival and awakening, including the first and second great awakenings.

✓ Laodicea represents the time from AD 1901 to our current time, which has been and continues to be a period of lukewarmness in the church and with a focus on creating wealth and abundance.

Based on this, we will be in the Laodicean age until the rapture of the church. This actually fits well with another prophetic marker that we see in 2 Thessalonians 2:3, "Don't let anyone deceive you in any way, for that day will not come until the rebellion occurs and the man of lawlessness is revealed, the man doomed to destruction." As mentioned previously, this word rebellion is translated from the Greek word apostasia, which is why some Bible translations use apostasy instead of rebellion. Both words are correct. It's a time when the church rebels and falls away. We are seeing much of that now in the rapidly growing deconstruction movement. Popular and well-known pastors and worship leaders are going public with their rejection of Jesus and Christianity or are a falling away from faith into sexual sin.

According to 2 Thessalonians, this must happen before the man of lawlessness, the antichrist is revealed. Plus, the antichrist cannot be revealed until the church is raptured, so we are very close to the rapture, when the church (all who accepted Jesus as their Savior) will rise up to meet Him in the air and go to live with Him forever (2 Thessalonians 4:16-17).

All that said, it's interesting that at the beginning of Revelation chapter four we read this in verse one, "After this I looked, and there before me was a door standing open in heaven. And the voice I had first heard speaking to me like a trumpet said, "Come up here, and I will show you what must take place after this." So, at the end of the church age, John is called into heaven by a voice and trumpet, which we also see in 2 Thessalonians 4:16-17 that describes the rapture of the church. I believe that when it's time for Jesus to come get the church, His bride, there will be a trumpet blast and a voice will shout come up and both the dead and alive believers will go up, in the twinkling of an eye to meet Jesus in the sky. I believe that Revelation 4:1 is Jesus showing John what is to come; the rapture of the church.

It is very clear that John is in the throne room of God during all of Revelation 4 and in verse 4, we see evidence that the church is in heaven with Jesus. Let's read Revelation 4:4, "Surrounding the throne were twenty-four other thrones, and seated on them were twenty-four elders. They were dressed in white and had crowns of gold on their heads." Notice that these are elders, which is a term only used in the Bible for people, so these could not be angels. They are also dressed in white. This is the Greek word leukos, which means bright or brilliant from whiteness. We might say dazzling white, which might remind us of Jesus when he was transfigured. Their clothing represents the new heavenly body all believers in Jesus receive when they die or are raptured. Now, I will admit that angels often are portrayed as dressed in bright white also, because they already have heavenly bodies. However, the next description, that they have crowns of gold on their head completely eliminates the idea that these could be angels. Gold crowns are a sign of royalty, which means these twenty-four elders must people.

The Bible doesn't say who these elders are, but they are sitting on thrones around God's throne and in Matthew 19:28 Jesus says, "Truly I tell you, at the renewal of all things, when the Son of Man sits on his glorious throne, you who have followed me will also sit on twelve thrones, judging the twelve tribes of Israel." So, to me, it's pretty clear that twelve of the twenty-four are the twelve disciples, which would mean that the church is in heaven before the tribulation begins, because in Revelation 5, Jesus takes the scroll and is the only one in heaven or on earth who can open the seven seals. Then in Revelation 6:1, Jesus opens the first seal, and the antichrist is revealed. The church is already in heaven before this happens, which requires a pre-tribulation rapture.

It's also good to notice the symbolic nature of the chapters of Revelation. In chapters 2 and 3, as I mentioned earlier, we see the church age and Jesus' messages to the church. In chapter 4, John is taking up into heaven symbolizing the rapture. Chapters 5-19 show us the seven-year tribulation and in chapter 19, Jesus returns to earth. The church is mentioned in chapters 1-3, but not mentioned or shown at all in chapters 5-18, because the church is in heaven with Jesus during the tribulation. The church shows up again in chapter 19 accompanying Jesus as He returns to earth. Some people say that these are angels following Jesus and they will definitely be among those following Jesus out of heaven. However, in verse 14, the armies of heaven are described as dressed in the finest of pure white linen, like the elders mentioned in chapter four.

The armies of heaven coming back with Jesus are wearing the finest of pure white linen, which might remind us of a wedding dress and since the church is the bride of Christ who is coming to a wedding and wedding feast, this would be appropriate. That means that the church was in heaven with Jesus seeing the place He prepared for her and preparing for the wedding. I will go into more detail on this in the next chapter.

There is one final and often missed piece of this part of the puzzle. Let's go to Revelation 1:20, "The mystery of the seven stars that you saw in my right hand and of the seven golden lampstands is this: The seven stars are the angels of the seven churches, and the seven lampstands are the seven churches." Note that the seven golden lampstands represent the seven churches, or we could say all churches and the church age. Then in chapters 2 and 3, Jesus gives letters to John for the seven churches. Now, let's turn to Revelation 4, where Jesus calls for John to come up to meet Him in heaven, a type and shadow of the rapture of the church. John is now in heaven, whether in the body or out of the body we don't know. But he sees the throne room of God and there, in verse 5 we read, "From the throne came flashes of lightning, rumblings and peals of thunder. In front of the throne, seven lamps were blazing. These are the seven spirits of God." The seven lamps, which represented the seven churches in chapter one, are now in heaven, in front of the throne and they are blazing.

What does that mean? Filled with the Holy Spirit or the seven spirits of God. We can understand these seven spirits from Isaiah 11:1-2 NASB1995, "Then a shoot will spring from the stem of Jesse, and a branch from his roots will bear fruit. The Spirit of the Lord will rest on Him, the spirit of wisdom and understanding, the spirit of counsel and strength, the spirit of knowledge and the fear of the

Lord." The shoot from the stem of Jesse is Jesus and the branch from his roots is anyone who has received Jesus as their Savior. The seven spirits are the seven expressions of the one Holy Spirit – Spirit of the Lord, Spirit of Wisdom, Spirit of Understanding, Spirit of Counsel, Spirit of Strength, Spirit of Knowledge, and Spirit of the Fear of the Lord. We, the church, have the Holy Spirit living in us.

Okay, so let's recap. Before the letters to the churches, the lampstands, representing those seven churches (but also all of the church), are on earth, but after John is called to heaven by Jesus (representing the rapture of the church), the lampstands and the Holy Spirit in them, are in heaven. All of this happens before Jesus opens the first seal, releasing the antichrist who initiates the seven-year tribulation by negotiating a peace treaty with Israel.

All of this is solid evidence for a pre-tribulation rapture.

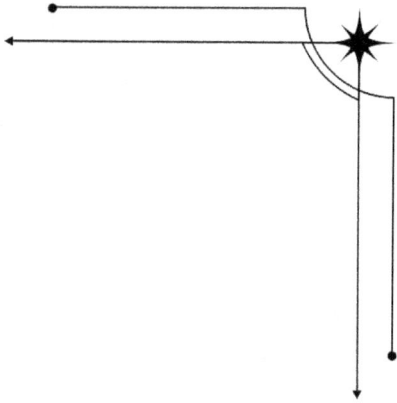

CHAPTER 7

THE BRIDE AND THE BRIDEGROOM

When describing the church, the Bible often uses wedding terminology and parables. Let's look at a few of these:

- ✓ Matthew 9:15, "Jesus answered, "How can the guests of the bridegroom mourn while he is with them? The time will come when the bridegroom will be taken from them; then they will fast." Jesus is saying that there will be a wedding, and He will be the groom, but first, he must be taken away from his bride.
- ✓ 2 Corinthians 11:2, "I am jealous for you with a godly jealousy. I promised you to one husband, to Christ, so that I might present you as a pure virgin to him." Paul is teaching the church in Corinth that they (the

church) are to be a pure bride to Jesus, the bridegroom.

✓ Matthew 22:2, "The kingdom of heaven is like a king who prepared a wedding banquet for his son." Here Jesus is referring to the wedding supper of the Lamb, which will follow the wedding between Jesus and the church.

✓ Matthew 22:12, "'He asked, 'How did you get in here without wedding clothes, friend?' The man was speechless.' But the man had no reply." This describes a person who arrives at the wedding without fine linen wedding clothes, which represent Jesus' righteousness that we receive when we accept Him as our Savior. No one will be allowed into heaven without wedding clothes, which represent the glorified body all believers receive when they die or are raptured.

✓ Matthew 25 – there is also the parable of the ten bridesmaids or virgins. You can go read it yourself. It shows some of what we are talking about in this chapter. The groom has gone away, and the bride and wedding party are preparing for his return. Some are prepared and some are not.

✓ John 3:29, "The bride belongs to the bridegroom. The friend who attends the bridegroom waits and listens for him and is full of joy when he hears the bridegroom's voice. That joy is mine, and it is now complete." This again refers to Jesus as the bridegroom and the church as the bride. There are different thoughts as to who the friends or guests will be, but I'm not going to address that in this book, as it's not important for the topic I'm covering.

As you can see there is clear connection between Jesus, the bridegroom and the church, the bride. Although this symbolism isn't as clear to us today, it would have been quite clear to the people of that day. Plus, the story of the bridegroom and the bride is a perfect type and shadow for the pre-tribulation rapture and the return of Jesus with His bride to earth. So, let's review the traditional Jewish wedding of that day and how it relates to Jesus as the bridegroom and the church as the bride.

A Jewish wedding was typically arranged by the fathers of the bride and groom. The groom's father would make an arrangement with the bride and her family and pay a significant bride price. The bride and her family would have to accept and once that was completed, the couple were betrothed.

Now, think about all believers as the bride, God as the father, and Jesus as the groom. Father God negotiated a bridal arrangement and offered a significant bride price, the life of His Son. When we accept the offer (grace) and receive Jesus as our Savior, we are also accepting Him as our groom and are betrothed. That is the state of the wedding today. We are now waiting for our groom to come back and get us to see the place He has been building, then the wedding, and the wedding feast.

Once the bride price has been paid and the agreement signed by the families, the groom then goes to his father's house and builds an addition for him and his bride to live. This would often take a year or more. In the meantime, the bride is preparing for the return of her groom and watching with great anticipation for him to return.

In John 14:1-3, Jesus says, "Do not let your hearts be troubled. You believe in God; believe also in me. My Father's house has many rooms; if that were not so, would I have told you that I am going there to prepare a place for you? And if I go and prepare a place for you, I will come back and take you to be with me that you also may be where I am." Jesus told all of His disciples (including us) that He was going to the Father's house to prepare a place for us. When it is ready He will come back and take us to be with him.

Back to the traditional Jewish wedding. The groom's father would watch the progress of the place the groom was preparing for his bride. When it was appropriately ready, the father would send his son to get the bride. So, only the father knew when the groom would come. The groom and bride did not know.

Now let's look at Matthew 24:36, "But about that day or hour no one knows, not even the angels in heaven, nor the Son, but only the Father." Jesus was speaking of when He would come to get His bride. Only the Father knows when.

Once the place was completed, the father would send the groom to get his bride. It would typically be in the middle of the night with shouting and trumpets blowing. He would come and snatch his bride away and take her to the place he had been preparing for her. The bride would have to be ready and watching for her groom.

We, believers in Jesus, also known as the bride of Christ, are preparing ourselves for the sudden return of our groom. Earlier we looked at 2 Corinthians 11:2, "For I am jealous for you with the jealousy of God himself. I promised you as a pure bride to one husband—Christ." While Jesus is away preparing a place for us, we are to allow the Holy Spirit to guide us in purification – getting rid of sin and rebellious thoughts and actions.

One day soon, Jesus, our bridegroom, will come back with a shout and trumpet blast. Believers in Jesus who have died, will be snatched away first to meet Him in the sky and then those who are still alive will join them in the sky. Jesus will then take His bride into heaven to the place He has been preparing. What an amazing moment that will be for all those who believe and have been preparing.

Now there are some critics who like to say that since God is not going to remove and protect the believers in the Old Testament or those who come to know the Lord during the tribulation, why would He do that with the church. Our typical answer is because He loves the bride. Their response is, but doesn't God love everyone? Yes, He does, but His love for the bride of Christ is different. Just as in this life, we can only legally have one bride, it's the same for Jesus. He can only have one bride and that would be all who believe in and receive Him as their Savior between when He ascended into heaven after His death and resurrection and when He will receive His bride in the sky. All those people are considered to be the church or Jesus' bride. Yes, God loves all those who followed His ways in the Old Testament. He loves those who come to know Jesus during the tribulation. None of those are considered to be the bride and so they will not be removed to marry the Bridegroom.

The Jewish wedding tradition clearly shows the rapture of the church – the snatching up of the one bride from the earth and into the place Jesus has prepared. The only question is when does this happen – before, in the middle of, or at the end of the seven-year tribulation? The Jewish wedding tradition doesn't give us an answer to that question, but if we look at the character of Father God, it's a pretty easy answer.

I am the father of three daughters who all enjoyed beautiful weddings. My wife and I wanted the very best we could offer. We wanted the weddings to be perfect and memorable, because we love our daughters. Now, if I had been presented with the idea that a terrible time was going to happen and I had the choice of removing my daughters before that time, in the middle, or at the end, I would, of course, choose to remove them before it happened. I would not want them to have to experience that terrible time, even if I could protect them during it. I would want them removed before it started and I am nothing compared to Father God. He too will make sure that His Son's bride is removed before anything terrible happens during the tribulation. That is the only answer that fits His character. This requires a pre-tribulation rapture of the church, the bride.

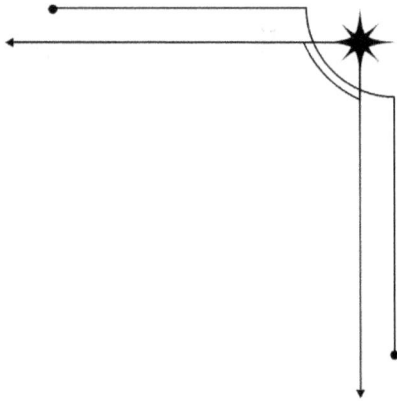

CHAPTER 8

THE NATURE AND CHARACTER OF GOD

There is a lot of solid biblical evidence for the rapture and the pre-tribulation timing, but in this chapter, I want to discuss the nature and character of God in relationship to the rapture and it's timing. The reason this is important to our decision making is that God is immutable, which means that He us unchanging and constant. Given that attribute, we can look at how God did things in the past and get a good idea of how He will handle things in the future. Let's start with some of His attributes and then we can look at how that plays out in the rapture scenario.

Love

1 John 4:8 says, "Whoever does not love does not know God, because God is love." God is love.

It's who He is, not something He does, so ever action is motivated by love. Now, I know what you are thinking. What about all His wrath in the Old Testament and then again during the tribulation? Actually, if you study all the wrath stories, you will always see that the foundation is love. He gives plenty of opportunities to repent for rebellion before He poured out His wrath. He will do that again all throughout the tribulation. So, how does His love play out in the rapture? I see two ways.

First, is His love for His bride, the church. I covered this extensively in chapter six, so I won't spend any more time here, except to reinforce that I can't imagine that God, as Father and Bridegroom, would want the church to experience even one moment of the tribulation. Now, God does allow us to experience normal life tribulation, but that isn't His wrath, which will be showcased in Old Testament fashion during the entire tribulation. But I don't believe He will allow the church to experience His wrath (for reasons explained earlier).

Second, is His love for all those who come to know Jesus during the tribulation. Much like during the church age, God doesn't just rapture them out of the earth the moment they receive Jesus as their Savior. They will have to endure the tribulation, but I believe based on both scripture and His proven character from the Old Testament, God will supernaturally protect tribulation believers from His wrath. Unfortunately, they will not be protected from the wrath of the antichrist and the devil. That is a consequence of making the choice to ignore the rapture warnings and refusing to receive Jesus prior to when God takes the bride into the sky to meet her Groom. God still loves the tribulation believers and there will still be a place for them in heaven and in the millennial kingdom. They will just have to endure a little longer. So, if you are one of those who has not yet received Jesus as your Savior, do it now. If you already have, make sure your friends and family have that opportunity before the rapture happens and that could be any moment now.

Justice

God is fair and impartial. Contrary to how scripture sounds, God doesn't select some people to be saved and others to reject. Jesus died for everyone, and so salvation is available to all of us, no matter how rebellious we have been. The moment we turn from our rebellion, God is right there to receive us, as we receive Him.

All that said, God is also Holy and His holiness and sin can't exist together. That's why when Adam and Eve sinned, out of love, He had to remove them from the Garden of Eden and He could no longer walk and talk with them without His holiness killing them. We see a great example of that in 2 Samuel 6:6-7, "When they came to the threshing floor of Nakon, Uzzah reached out and took hold of the ark of God, because the oxen stumbled. The Lord's anger burned against Uzzah because of his irreverent act; therefore, God struck him down, and he died there beside the ark of God." Wow, all Uzzah did was try to steady the ark and God zapped him dead. Why? Because the ark held the presence and holiness of God and it reacted badly to Uzzah's sinful touch.

The good news is that Father God developed a way for us to be in relationship with Him again. He sacrificed His own Son, Jesus, in our place, as a legal substitute for all of the sin of humanity. The blood sacrifice neutralized our sin. God's justice was served on the cross. However, God doesn't force it on everyone. Rather, He offers it as a gift to be received. Many have already received, but many more have not and at the time of the rapture, that fact will become very clear. Those who have decided to go their own way and not accept God's gift of salvation, will have to endure part or all of the horrible tribulation. That's justice and if God were not just, then anyone could get into heaven, and it would be just as terrible as earth. I don't want a heaven full of sin, violence, sickness, and death. How about you?

I'm sure that, like me, you've made some bad decisions in your life and had to live with the consequences. Earlier in my life, I made a lot of bad financial decisions that resulted in me having to declare bankruptcy. If that wasn't bad enough, I did it again and was $120,000 in consumer debt in the year 2000. However, that time I sought the Lord's wisdom, did what He said to do, and in 2005 all that debt was paid off.

Because of justice, there are consequences to our actions. Fortunately, we don't always get what we deserve. When I was a teenager, I started the poor hobby of shoplifting and got caught. The police were called, and they took me to my home to get my mom and then back to the store. Fortunately, because of my sincere repentance, I wasn't charged. I didn't get what I deserved.

God's justice system is the same. We deserve eternal torture in the fires of hell, but because Jesus took our sins and died on the cross, we don't get what we deserve. We get grace. God's full grace extends until the rapture of the church and then His grace is more like that seen in the Old Testament. Again, make the decision to stop your rebellion and receive Jesus now.

Mercy

Throughout the entire Bible, we see that God is merciful. Let's start with Adam and Eve. God creates the perfect earth and places them in a perfect paradise. They are instructed to eat from any tree except the tree of the knowledge of good and evil. Keep in mind that they did not have the sin nature we have and had never thought or experienced evil; only good. That was God's intention for His kids. He did not want them to ever have to experience evil. Then along comes the snake, the devil, satan, who deceives them into rebelling against God by eating from that forbidden tree. Instead of God getting angry, killing them, and starting over, He lovingly has them removed from the garden to live in a now tainted earth. Why do I say lovingly? Because if God had left them in the garden, they could have eaten from the tree of life and lived forever. What's so bad about living forever? Think about what it would be like living with the guilt and shame they must have felt and the separation from

God? That's hard during a normal lifetime, but how about for eternity? God loved them too much to allow for that, so He would not allow them access to the tree of life. Also, because they were ashamed of their nakedness, He killed animals and made clothing. That was the first animal sacrifice to cover sin.

Another great example is Noah. God created the universe, including the earth, then formed a man, Adam, out of the dirt and breathed life into him. From the man, God took a rib and formed a woman, Eve, to be Adam's wife. They lived in paradise and walked and talked with God. But, as we know, the rebelled against God and were sent out into the world. That all happened in chapters 1 through 3 of Genesis and by chapter 6, humankind was so evil that God decided to destroy them all with a flood. However, He found one righteous man, named Noah.

Ps 37:28 NKJV says, "For the Lord loves justice, And does not forsake His saints." A saint is a person who is following God and living a godly life. That was Noah, so although God was going to pour out His justice on the earth, he was not going to forsake Noah and his family. You know the story- God gave Noah instructions to build a huge boat. According to the Ark Encounter, the ark was 510 feet long, 85 feet wide, and 51 feet high and it was built at a time when there were no power tools. Although the Bible doesn't say how long it took Noah to build the ark, we can estimate it to be around 75 years. Imagine the faith it took to invest over seven decades of your life to build a boat in the middle of the desert at a time when it had never rained? God honored that faith by removing the righteous saint from the place where His wrath was poured out. The ark was literally taken by the water higher than the mountain peaks, so they were above the wrath of God. During the rapture, the saints who followed Jesus, both dead and living, will rise up to meet Him in the sky and be above God's wrath.

Another good example that shows God's character is Lot, who was Abraham's nephew. When God told Abram (his name was later changed to Abraham) to leave his home and go to the land God was giving him, Lot went with him. Over time, God prospered them both and so they separated, and Lot began to live in a city called Sodom. This was a very evil city with people like those in the days of Noah and similar to the way things are in present day. But Lot was a righteous man and so once again, God would love justice but not forsake His saint. God sent two angels to bring Lot and his family out of Sodom and into the high country, above Sodom, before the city was destroyed by God's wrath. It's God's character to be just, but also merciful to the saints.

God is the same yesterday, today, and tomorrow, so we can know based on His character and the way He has done things in the past, that God will remove the church, Jesus' bride from the earth, before the seven-year tribulation begins, when He will pour out His wrath.

Again, more evidence for a pre-tribulation rapture.

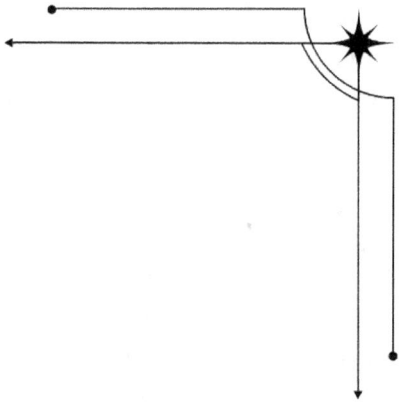

CHAPTER 9

JACOB'S TROUBLE

The prophet Jeremiah gave a prophetic word in Jeremiah 30:3 that God's people, Israel, and Judah would return to the land God game them and possess it. That happened in 1948. Later in Jeremiah 30:5-7 NKJV, the prophet says that there will be a future time of great trembling and fear. It will be a time like no other and Jeremiah refers to it as the time of Jacob's trouble (NKJV). But the prophet assures the Jewish people that they will be saved out of it.

Many theologians believe that the time of Jacob's trouble is the seven-year tribulation and that the focus of that time is to get the Jewish people saved. Although the Bible doesn't explicitly say this, there is much evidence for this concept. Let's look at some of it.

First, Revelation chapters 4 through the first half of 19 are very Jewish sounding. There are over four hundred references to the Jewish people and the Old Testament.

Second, are the 144,000 that we see in Revelation 7:1-8, "After this I saw four angels standing at the four corners of the earth, holding back the four winds of the earth to prevent any wind from blowing on the land or on the sea or on any tree. Then I saw another angel coming up from the east, having the seal of the living God. He called out in a loud voice to the four angels who had been given power to harm the land and the sea: 'Do not harm the land or the sea or the trees until we put a seal on the foreheads of the servants of our God.' Then I heard the number of those who were sealed: 144,000 from all the tribes of Israel. From the tribe of Judah 12,000 were sealed, from the tribe of Reuben 12,000, from the tribe of Gad 12,000, from the tribe of Asher 12,000, from the tribe of Naphtali 12,000, from the tribe of Manasseh 12,000, from the tribe of Simeon 12,000, from the tribe of Levi 12,000, from the tribe of Issachar 12,000, from the tribe of Zebulun 12,000, from the tribe of Joseph 12,000, from the tribe of Benjamin 12,000.

Clearly these 144,000 men are Jewish. They are sealed by God, which means they are protected by God. They are referred to as servants, which means God is using them during the tribulation. Very likely, they are super apostles like Paul preaching the gospel boldly to the Jewish people who were left behind in the rapture. Now, there will also be non-Jewish people who will hear their teaching and receive Jesus too. This is a big-time revival going on during the tribulation, as God saves His chosen people, the Jews.

Third, are the two supernatural witnesses that we find in Revelation 11:3-6, "And I will appoint my two witnesses, and they will prophesy for 1,260 days, clothed in sackcloth." They are "the two olive trees" and the two lampstands, and "they stand before the Lord of the earth." If anyone tries to harm them, fire comes from their mouths and devours their enemies. This is how anyone who wants to harm them must die. They have power to shut up the heavens so that it will not rain during the time they are prophesying; and they have power to turn the waters into blood and to strike the earth with every kind of plague as often as they want."

These two witnesses are referred to as two olive trees. Zechariah prophesied about them in Zechariah 4:14. Olive trees were used in the temple to provide olive oil to burn in the lampstands in the Jewish temples. Because of this and what they do, many Bible scholars think that Moses and Elijah will be the two witnesses. Others think it will be Enoch and Elijah, because both were taken alive into heaven. Either way, the primary audience of their teaching are the Jewish people and again, many will get saved during the tribulation.

Jesus teaches about the times leading up to and about the tribulation itself in Matthew 24. He refers to the abomination that causes desolation that will be set up in the third Jewish temple, which will be built either just prior to the tribulation or during the first half. Jesus says that once they see the abomination of desolation, they should flee to the mountains and tells them to pray that it won't be in winter (because only the Father knows when Jesus, the bridegroom, will come back) or during the Sabbath. Clearly Jesus was speaking to future Jews because Gentiles don't officially observe the Sabbath.

Although the tribulation is not totally about the Jews, they are the primary focus. Many rejected Jesus when He was on earth teaching and healing and many continue to reject Him as their Savior. Those Jews who have received Jesus as their Savior are part of the church/bride. However, many will be left behind, and God's focus will be to get them to repent and recognize their Messiah, Jesus.

In Zechariah chapters 12 and 13, we see a lot of Messianic prophesies, including his death by piercing. Then in 13:8-9 we see a prophecy about Israel and the tribulation, "In the whole land," declares the Lord, "two-thirds will be struck down and perish; yet one-third will be left in it. This third I will put into the fire; I will refine them like silver and test them like gold. They will call on my name and I will answer them; I will say, 'They are my people,' and they will say, 'The Lord is our God.'" This leads us to believe that only one third of the Jewish population will survive the tribulation and that it is a time to refining by fire. Now, in the two-thirds who die during the tribulation, many may have become believers because of the preaching of the 144,000 and the two witnesses.

Because the tribulation seems to have such a Jewish focus, rather than a church focus, it would lead us to believe that the church is not present during the tribulation. That would require a pre-tribulation rapture.

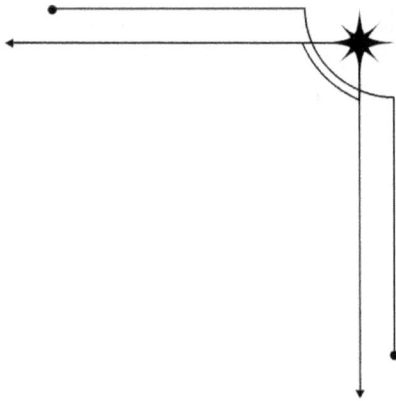

CHAPTER 10

ESCAPE

There are many out there who teach that the pre-tribulation rapture is just escapism. The reason they say this is because they equate normal life troubles with what happens in the tribulation and say that God doesn't allow believers to escape the normal troubles of life, so why would He allow them to escape the tribulation. They view it as avoiding suffering and responsibility.

Before we get into that, let's look at what Jesus had to say in Luke 21:36 NKJV, "Watch therefore, and pray always that you may be counted worthy to escape all these things that will come to pass, and to stand before the Son of Man." Seems to me that Jesus is encouraging escapism.

Okay, let's go back to the issue of normal life struggles and what happens during the tribulation.

The troubles we experience in this life, no matter how bad, are not the wrath of God. Right now, His wrath is held back by the sacrificial blood of Jesus represented in the church. Believers will suffer in this fallen world just like everyone else.

Second, if God wants to remove Jesus' bride from the earth before He pours out His terrible wrath, who wouldn't want to escape? I have to laugh when I hear people say that they want to be left behind to face the antichrist. No, you don't. That said, we should prepare ourselves in prayer and the Word for the trials and tribulations of this world, as they are undoubtedly going to get bad before the rapture of the church.

Third, critics of the pre-tribulation rapture often say that pre-trib teaches that believers won't suffer during the end times. We are very sheltered here in the United States, but in other parts of the world, it's so bad that people may think they are in the tribulation, but they aren't. I believe that even here in the U.S. there will be greater persecution and suffering as we approach the rapture of the church. Critics think that because of the escapist mentality of the pre-tribulation rapture, believers will not be prepared for persecution and suffering. On the contrary, Jesus teaches us to be ready and watching for Him. It's up to us to be prepared for whatever comes, no matter what our belief in the timing of the rapture.

Fourth, critics say that the pre-tribulation is a theology of comfort over challenge, but actually it's just the opposite. In Luke 19:13 Jesus teaches us to occupy until he comes. In Mark 16:15, Jesus commands us to go into all the world and preach the gospel. Then in Matthew 28:19-20 Jesus gives what is known as the great commission, to go and make disciples of all nations. These are not suggestions and those who believe in a pre-tribulation rapture are more motivated to do all these things, because they don't want people to be left behind to endure the tribulation.

Fifth, critics say that those who believe in a pre-tribulation rapture are detached and disconnected, just waiting for Jesus to come get them. I've met and heard teachings from hundreds of people who believe in pre-tribulation rapture, and they are the most connected. They are out sharing the gospel, running for political office or school board, teaching and writing books, and planting churches in homes and buildings.

What I love about people who believe in the pre-tribulation rapture is that they seem to have greater hope in this dark world. They have more joy and are less critical of others. They are following hard after Jesus and bringing as many with them as they can. They are connected and doing the work Jesus said to do.

The Apostle Paul, in his teaching about the rapture in 1 Thessalonians 4:13-18, ends the teaching with this statement, "Therefore encourage one another with these words." The only rapture scenario that allows for this to be completely true is the pre-tribulation rapture. All the others require the church to go through half, most, or all of the horrible tribulation. That's not very encouraging. That's why I believe that those who believe in the pre-trib rapture are those who are most encouraged and are out doing the stuff Jesus said to do.

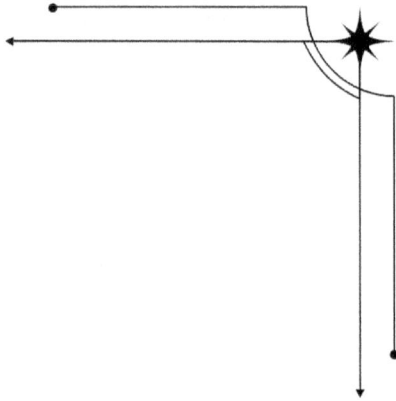

CHAPTER 11

DEBUNKING MYTHS AND MISINFORMATION

Because of all that is happening in the world, there is probably more teaching and books being published about the end times and the rapture than any other single topic. Anyone can set up a YouTube channel and become an "expert." In Matthew 24, Jesus warned about false prophets who will deceive many in the end times. 2 Peter 2:1 says that there will be false teachers who will secretly "introduce destructive heresies, even denying the sovereign Lord who bought them." In verse 3 it says about these false teachers, "In their greed these teachers will exploit you with fabricated stories." In 1 Timothy 4:1 it tells us, "The Spirit clearly says that in later times some will abandon the faith and follow deceiving spirits and things taught by demons." I believe there are some of the end times teachings that would fall into this category, so in this chapter I'm going to debunk some of the myths and misinformation about the pre-tribulation rapture.

Secret Event

There are some pre-tribulation critics who talk about the rapture like it's a secret event with a select group of Christians who go. First, it's not a special group of elite Christians, everyone who has believed in and received Jesus as their personal Savior, will go in the rapture. Second, this will be a very loud and public event that everyone in the world will experience one way or another.

Let's look at the primary rapture scripture 1 Thessalonians 4:15-17, "According to the Lord's word, we tell you that we who are still alive, who are left until the coming of the Lord, will certainly not precede those who have fallen asleep. For the Lord himself will come down from heaven, with a loud command, with the voice of the archangel and with the trumpet call of God, and the dead in Christ will rise first. After that, we who are still alive and are left will be caught up together with them in the clouds to meet the Lord in the air. And so we will be with the Lord forever."

A quick side note is that Paul says, "According to the Lord's word," so this is not something Paul made up, or he heard from another person, rather he heard it directly from Jesus. Next, take notice in verse 16 that "the Lord himself will come down from heaven, with a loud command, with the voice of the archangel and with the trumpet call of God." This is going to be loud and everyone will hear it – a loud command from the voice of the archangel – this could be Gabriel, the messenger, or perhaps Michael, the war angel. That is followed by the trumpet call of God, and you know that's going to be loud!

No, this will not be a secret event in any way. It will be a loud trumpet call that we will not be able to miss and then billions of people will disappear from the earth.

No Direct Scripture References for a Pre-Tribulation Rapture

The truth is there aren't any direct scripture references for the pre-tribulation rapture, but then again, there aren't any for any of the other theories either. Yet, we know that there will be a rapture. I believe that, in this book, I presented enough solid evidence for the pre-tribulation rapture that a judge would rule in my favor. It's also important to recognize that there are many concepts in the Bible that don't have direct scripture references. For example, we can see the trinity represented, but there are no scriptures that use the word trinity or speak directly of the triune God.

Just because there is no direct scriptural reference, doesn't mean it doesn't exist. It just means that we need to look at the whole collection of scripture to properly interpret. When we do that, it's overwhelming that the timing of the rapture will be pre-tribulation.

Saints in the Tribulation (Rev 13:7)

Critics of the pre-tribulation rapture say that the church is present during the tribulation, which is a topic I delt with earlier in the book. The scripture they use is Revelation 13:7 NKJV, "It was granted to him to make war with the saints and to overcome them. And authority was given him over every tribe, tongue, and nation." The critics say that these saints must be the church, but they forget to look at the whole compilation of scripture.

The word saints is not an exclusive word for the church. In the NKJV, the word "saints" appears in Deuteronomy 33:2-3, 1 Samuel 2:9, 2 Chronicles 6:41, Job 15:15, Psalm 16:3, Psalm 30:4 and many other Old Testament scriptures. Clearly these saints were not part of the church, but they do reference people who are following God and that is who the saints are in Revelation 13:7. They are people who receive Jesus as their Savior during the tribulation.

Matthew 24 Teaching of Post-Trib Rapture

The mid-trib, pre-wrath, and post-trib people all use Matthew 24 to support their theory. It's not possible for Matthew 24 to support all three theories. I discussed Matthew 24 earlier in the book and the best way to understand it is to see that it refers to both the rapture of the church and the return of Jesus to earth. I delt with the interpretation of Matthew 24 in Chapter 4, so if you still have questions about this, go back and review that chapter.

One addition is that in Matthew 24:40 the Greek word that is translated as taken is paralambano, which is the same Greek word used in John 14:3, when Jesus talks about taking His disciples (rapture) to the place where He is going. Jesus is in heaven preparing a place for His church/bride. At the rapture, Jesus will come down and the bride will meet Him in the sky to be escorted by the Bridegroom to a new heavenly home.

So, although many try to teach that Matthew 24 is about the second coming, it is really about both the rapture and the second coming, which are all one event in two parts (more on that later).

Recent Theory Not Held by the Early Church

This is very commonly used, particularly by the mid- and post-tribulation advocates. They like to say that the pre-tribulation rapture theory was developed by John Nelson Darby in the 1830's. I also discussed this in Chapter 4 and proved through the teachings of multiple early church leaders that they taught about the pre-tribulation rapture a thousand years before Darby.

Contradicts the Bible Theme of Suffering

Those people who try to use this to discredit the pre-tribulation theory say that the Bible constantly shows followers of God and Jesus who suffer persecution, troubles, and hardship. This is true, because we live in a fallen world with evil people and we make bad choices. That said, the only places we see followers of God experiencing His wrath is in the Old Testament and during the seven-year tribulation. We don't see God's wrath poured out in any way during the church age; the time between the day of Pentecost, when the Holy Spirit was poured out and the rapture of the church.

Yes, believers suffered during the church age. Jesus died on the cross. All of the disciples except John were martyred for their faith. In our time millions of Christians have been persecuted and killed for their faith, but again, this is the wrath of man, not the wrath of God.

Only One Second Coming

Post-tribulation people like to say that there is only one second coming and it happens at the end of the tribulation. They would be right. The only time that Jesus actually comes back and sets foot on the earth is at the end of the tribulation. We see this prophetically in Zechariah 14:4, "On that day his feet will stand on the Mount of Olives, east of Jerusalem, and the Mount of Olives will be split in two from east to west, forming a great valley, with half of the mountain moving north and half moving south."

That is the second coming of Christ, but it's very different from what we see in 1 Thessalonians 4:16-17, "For the Lord himself will come down from heaven, with a loud command, with the voice of the archangel and with the trumpet call of God, and the dead in Christ will rise first. After that, we who are still alive and are left will be caught up together with them in the clouds to meet the Lord in the air. And so we will be with the Lord forever." Here we see those who are "in Christ," which means those who have received Jesus as their Savior, both dead and alive meeting Jesus in the air and going to be where He is, in heaven. This clearly shows two very different events – the rapture of the church and the return of Christ.

Separation of Israel and the Church

Many of those who support other rapture theories try to say that those who believe in the pre-tribulation theory have either replaced Israel with the church (replacement theology) or that God is taking the church out of the way, so He can go back to His work on His chosen people, the Jews.

First, the church includes both Jews and gentiles, so those who are raptured prior to the seven-year tribulation will be from both Israel and the church. Second, there is no support for the church replacing Israel. God still has a plan for the Jewish people, and He shows that heavily in the tribulation with the 144,000 Jewish super apostles and many other Jewish references.

Everything in Revelation already happened around AD 70

There are some people, referred to as preterists, who believe that everything we read about in Revelation happened around AD 70 when the Romans destroyed Jerusalem and the temple. This is not a widely held view in the church and conflicts with the teachings of the early church leaders The biggest fault with this view is that it says that Jesus already returned to the earth and we are living under his reign on earth. I don't know about you, but in my seven decades on earth, I've never seen Jesus in the person. The main reason people believe this is because of Jesus' statement in Matthew 24:34, "Truly I tell you, this generation will certainly not pass away until all these things have happened." Jesus was describing things that happen in the tribulation and the interpretation by preterists is that He was talking about that generation of people. Jesus was talking about the generation that would see the things He was describing and that is our current generation. The rapture is close, spread the word!

The gospel must be preached to every person before the rapture can occur.

The scripture often referenced is Matthew 24:14, when Jesus said, "And this gospel of the kingdom will be preached in the whole world as a testimony to all nations, and then the end will come." The end that Jesus was referring to is the end of the tribulation. We know this because during the seven-year tribulation there will be 144,000 Jewish apostles preaching the gospel, two super-natural witnesses also preaching the gospel for three and a half years, and finally an angel will fly across the sky, in full view of everyone, preaching the gospel. Then, Jesus will return to the earth and set up His Kingdom on earth for 1,000 years. Although there will be no non-believers who enter the millennium, there will be those believers who survive the tribulation in their human bodies. They will have children, who will have children, who will have children for 1,000 years. Those children will also have the opportunity to choose Jesus as their Savior or reject Him and face the white throne judgment at the end of the millennium.

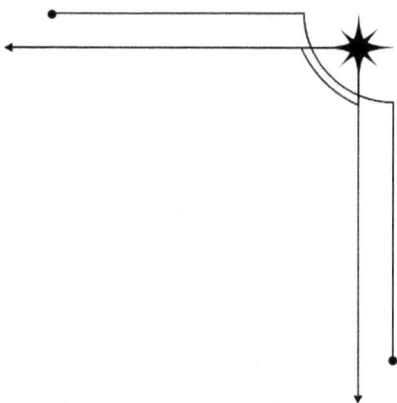

CHAPTER 12

THE WRAP UP

A s I wrap this up, let's do a quick recap. First, there doesn't seem to be any doubt that there is a rapture and that it is different than the second coming of Jesus. The only question is the timing of the rapture. As I've stated in this book, after over twenty years of studying scripture and developing a deep and intimate relationship with God, I'm convinced, without a shadow of doubt, that the rapture will happen before the seven-year tribulation begins. The following is a summary of why I believe that.

✓ There is a lot of historical support from both the Bible and the teachings of the early church leaders for the pre-tribulation rapture.

✓ The scriptures make it very clear that those who have received Jesus as their Savior are not appointed to wrath. In other words, the wrath that they deserved because of sin, was poured out on Jesus on the cross. God cannot then pour out His wrath on believers again.

✓ Jesus is the Bridegroom and all of those who have received Him as Savior are considered to be His bride. No groom would allow his bride to go through the horrific events that are part of the tribulation. Jesus is better than any other groom, so He will definitely come and get His bride before He opens the first seal.

✓ God's nature is such that sin requires justice in the form of wrath, but God poured out His wrath on Jesus for the church/bride. However, those who don't receive Jesus as their Savior will face wrath, both at death or if they are alive, during the tribulation. That said, God is also merciful and has proved it throughout history by removing the righteous people (such as Noah and Lot) before He poured out His wrath. That's His nature and He won't go against that nature with the rapture of the church.

✓ In the book of Revelation, we clearly see the church in heaven before Jesus, the Lamb of God, opens the first seal, which begins the pouring out of God's wrath.

✓ From Revelation four through the first part of nineteen are clearly very Jewish in nature. The church will be gone, so that God can finally bring the Jews into the saving knowledge of Jesus, their Messiah and He will go all out to save them, because of His love for His people.

✓ Jesus said that we should seek to be worth enough to escape what is coming (Luke 21:36). Who wouldn't want to escape the seven-year tribulation. However, the church cannot use that as a reason to get comfortable. We still have work to do and should use the imminence of the rapture to motivate us to share the gospel with everyone.

✓ The rapture is not some secret event for a secret group of people. It will be loud and noticeable by all, as millions or billions of people just disappear in an instant. The good news is that it is for all who receive Jesus as their Savior.

I believe that the scripture overwhelmingly supports the pre-tribulation rapture view. That said, I was directed by the Holy Spirit to write this book, not to prove that others are wrong, but purely to share the evidence I have seen in the scriptures and through my relationship with God, for a pre-tribulation rapture. I know that there are many out there who believe that they have evidence for one of the other theories. Feel free to read and study the other theories and make up your mind. But please do take a position, don't be one of those lazy pan-tribulation people who just figure that things will "pan out" in the end. You have an obligation to your family, friends, and all those around you to have an opinion on what is going to happen in these end times.

The good news is that the rapture is something we can agree or disagree about, and it won't affect the main thing, which is salvation. As long as we agree that we have all sinned and fallen short of the glory of God and need the sacrifice of Jesus to take care of our sin and put us into right relationship with God. That Jesus was resurrected to new life, so we can too. If we agree about that, then we are good to go.

None of us know for sure when the rapture will occur until that moment that we rise up to meet Jesus in the sky. Only the Father knows when He will send His Son back to earth. That said, based on all I see in the world today; I think we are close. Use the urgency of this world changing event to bring people to Jesus and into the Kingdom of God. Two good tools to accomplish this are my books *Where Did All the People Go?* and *SAVED*. You can find information on both books, and my other books on the following pages. Enjoy!

ABOUT THE AUTHOR

Rod Nichols was called by God out of a successful business career to launch ministries, plant churches, write books, and equip the body of Christ. He serves as the Executive and Teaching Pastor at AZ Vineyard Church in Goodyear, Arizona. Rod is also the founder of the True Disciple Academy, an online Bible school, which you can find at TrueDiscipleAcademy.com. He has published thirteen books, including *True Disciple*, *God's Financial Plan*, *Where Did All the People Go?* and *SAVED*.

OTHER BOOKS
BY ROD NICHOLS

Throughout the Bible we find ordinary, fallible people just like us. These ordinary people did extraordinary things. Then along came Jesus. He said that his followers would do even greater things than he did. A mind-blowing promise! Yet, most believers haven't experienced the miracles we see in God's Word. What is the difference between the people in the Bible and those sitting in any of our churches?

The answer to that question is found in Rod Nichols' new book, True Disciple. Rod believes the Lord instructed him to write his true disciple story. He was (and still is) one of those ordinary, fallible people that God taught to be a true disciple of Jesus Christ. Rod is real and transparent about his struggles, doubts, fears, questions, and failures. He shares some amazing adventures and what he learned along the way. With God's help, these lessons could transform any ordinary person into a mountain moving true disciple.

In True Disciple, Nichols hopes to motivate the church to love God with all they have and to love people as Jesus loved us; to get out from those comfy seats and secure walls and go do what Jesus commanded - preach the gospel to the world, make disciples, heal, deliver, and help those in need. Are you ready for the adventure of a lifetime? Would you like to have God use you to change the world around you? True Disciple will prepare you for an amazing journey!

Order on Amazon

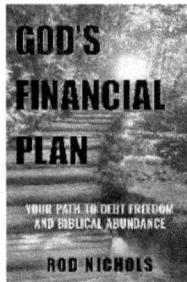

GOD'S
FINANCIAL
PLAN
YOUR PATH TO DEBT FREEDOM
AND BIBLICAL ABUNDANCE
ROD NICHOLS

Are you experiencing debt and financial struggles? Does it feel hopeless at times? Well, it's not, because God has a financial plan for you. All you have to do is learn about and implement the plan in your life. That's what the author, Rod Nichols, did. He and his wife were $120,000 in debt, feeling lost and hopeless. Yet, after entering into God's financial plan, they were debt free in just five years and have remained so to this day.

God did not create you to be poor and to struggle financially. He created you to live the abundant life that Jesus died for. He created you to help finance the growth of the His Kingdom here on earth. He created you to prosper in every part of your life, which includes finances.

In this book, Rod Nichols shares the scripture-based plan that God has for the financial lives of His children. He also shares practical tips that God gave him for getting out of debt and increasing your income. These are proven concepts that have worked for Rod and many others, and they will work for you.

It's time for you to get out of debt and begin enjoying biblical abundance.

Order God's Financial Plan on Amazon

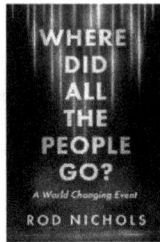

Depending on when you are reading this book, either millions, possibly billions of people have disappeared or will disappear soon. The world is or will be in total chaos as it enters the worst time in world history.

If this disappearance has not happened yet, then this book will unveil the future and give you instructions on what to do before people disappear. It's also a great book to share with family and friends, so they too can make the right decision, before it's too late.

If people have already disappeared, then this book will give you a clear and accurate picture of what will happen in the years to come. Read and study the book carefully, as you will have a second chance to make the right decision, but it will come at a cost.

For those who are living before the mass disappearance, leave copies of this book in your home, office, and vehicles, so that those who are left behind can read and understand what has happened and what is to come.

Order Where Did All the People Go? on Amazon

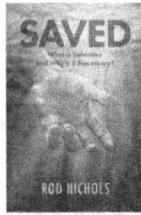

Salvation was a confusing topic for me, and for many others. I hear comments like, "I've lived a good life, so I should get into heaven" or "I've done more good than bad, so I'm sure I'll get into heaven" or "I'm a good person and good people go to heaven" or "hell is the place where all the fun people go." All of these are things that I once thought, or I've heard from other people. In this book, I share my rough road to salvation. I also answer what salvation is and why it's necessary.

If you are a church attender who wonders if you are really saved, this is the book for you. If you are a seeker, trying to find your way, you will love this book. If you are a follower of Christ and have friends who are not yet saved, this is a great book to get the conversation started. It's a quick and easy read, yet it's packed with the facts necessary to make a good eternal decision.

Order on Amazon

www.ingramcontent.com/pod-product-compliance
Lightning Source LLC
Chambersburg PA
CBHW070525030426
42337CB00016B/2105